LEARNING TO READ

The Quest for Meaning

LEARNING TO READ

The Quest for Meaning

Malcolm P. Douglass

Teachers College, Columbia University
New York and London

Published by Teachers College Press, 1234 Amsterdam Avenue
New York, NY 10027

Library of Congress Cataloging-in-Publication Data

Douglass, Malcolm P.
  Learning to read : the quest for meaning / Malcolm P. Douglass.
     p.   cm.
  Bibliography: p.
  Includes index.
  ISBN 0-8077-2970-1 (alk. paper)
  1. Reading—United States. I. Title.
LB1050.D66 1989   89-4999
372.6—dc20   CIP

ISBN 0-8077-2970-1

Manufactured in the United States of America

96 95 94 93 92 91 90 89   8 7 6 5 4 3 2 1

For Enid

Contents

Acknowledgments

I owe the opening quotation in Chapter 1 to Lil Thompson, former Headmistress of Birches Avenue Infant School on the outskirts of Wolverhampton, Staffordshire, England. Lil is a master teacher widely known in England, partly because the BBC has seen fit to make two television films of her work as a gifted teacher of young children, and partly through lectures delivered both in England and the United States over the past decade.

I wish to thank the following publishers for permission to reprint copyrighted materials in this book:

Figure 3.1, the National Reading Conference; Figure 3.2, Academic Press, for its journal, *Cognitive Psychology*; Figure 3.3, The National Council of Teachers of English; Figure 5.1, courtesy of Hans Furth; list ('Stages in Spelling Development') in Chapter 7, Houghton Mifflin Company.

Introduction

I began my career as a teacher at a time when little was known about the development of children's abilities to use language and, consequently, in a time of naive notions about the connection between teaching and learning where language acquisition was concerned. The assumption was that children learned to speak by imitating the language they heard around the house, directed mainly by the mother. That language development extended over a period of years in increasingly complex forms, and that its acquisition might be infinitely more complicated than the imitative or copycat model we assumed, and taught, seemed an unlikely prospect.

All that began to change during the sixties when a new tool fell into the hands of researchers interested in language acquisition. The high-fidelity tape recorder made it possible to study oral language in a way never before feasible because, unlike earlier audio-recorders, it could provide the highly accurate representation of speech needed to find pieces of language hitherto hidden from view.

At the same time, inquiry into the growth and development of children's thought processes identified a complementary avenue of knowledge. This knowledge, when linked with new information about the development of verbal language abilities, provided a theoretic base for understanding how children grow and learn, a view that stood in sharp contrast with the conventional wisdom. That wisdom, which I assimilated since none other was available for me to compare it with, asserted the unique nature of what I will designate here as reading words in their printed form (to distinguish this behavior as clearly as possible from other kinds of "reading," such as reading musical notation, reading mathematical symbols, even reading faces—all ways of knowing, the generic meaning of the term, *reading*).

The conventional wisdom holds that each of the verbal language functions—*speaking, listening, reading,* and *writing*—possesses distinctive characteristics learned in unique ways that consequently require specialized methods of teaching. The school's responsibility lies primarily in the teaching of reading and writing; major emphasis should be given to these areas because children acquire their oral language skills at home. The school's task thus should become focused on reading and subsequently, writing, both of which are learned through the acquisition of certain skills that are best taught didactically, directly, just as one would teach any other subject in the school curriculum. Although children may learn their oral language skills at home in a naturalistic setting, learning to read and write in school, it is argued, requires a different approach, or the requisite skills will never be learned.

Paralleling these assumptions was the predominant notion that the years preceding the advent of adolescence are ones of psychological and intellectual latency — basic skills are learned and consolidated during this period, but it is otherwise of no particular significance in the development of intellectual powers; real learning begins in earnest following the completion of elementary school.

Such thinking has led to certain conclusions about how teaching and learning should proceed. Since it was thought that the development of skill is prerequisite to reading, and thinking, teaching should be directed first at skill development. Further, because reading was considered a distinct subject in the school curriculum, the primary problems in the teaching of reading were thought to be the refinement of what that subject matter should be and the discovery of the most efficient ways of teaching it.

It was out of this kind of reasoning that the dominant form of instruction has emerged: reading taught as a subject in the school curriculum within a textbook format in which daily lessons have as their primary focus the acquisition of a predetermined skill or other subject matter element deemed essential to the learning-to-read process. Writing in this view need receive little attention beyond developing the ability to construct letters into words that are spelled "correctly." The problem of writing has been and is still largely seen as the development of the skills of fluency and accuracy; the content of children's writing has not attracted particular attention because, in this view, questions about original content are best postponed until the primary objective — development of the skill of representing language on paper in acceptable form — is attained and after thought processes are sufficiently mature.

Uneasiness over both the apparent simplicity of this view and its manifest failure to produce consistently positive results has been expressed for many years, at least since the late 1800s. Having to rely more on a sense that traditional practice was somehow wanting in fundamental ways, doubters such as myself were left to challenge the status quo with insufficient ammunition from research, a circumstance that now has altered dramatically. Additionally, of course, schools are by their very nature conservative institutions in which change comes about slowly, if at all. Even though another approach to instruction may appear at least equally effective, there is little incentive to change, since change always requires additional effort. Thus it is that the status quo endures.

In this book, the reader will find a bias stemming from a personal value orientation about the nature of learning and the purposes to be served by education, a bias that I believe is increasingly being supported by research. It is my contention that traditional practice in the teaching of reading is, at best, extraordinarily inefficient. While many children learn to read where instruction is based on teaching a particular subject matter of skills and other specific behaviors associated with what we think of as mature reading behavior, we have no direct evidence of a cause and effect. That is, we do not know whether they learn to read *because of*, or *in spite of*, the instruction provided in such classrooms. What we can be sure of is that there are too many children who do not learn to either read fluently or write well. In this book, I will explore the various dimensions of reading behavior in order to develop a conceptual framework for thinking of it in its totality, and then extrapolate what this may mean for teaching and learning. Finally, I will look at some of the sources of difficulty individuals and society encounter on the road to literacy.

I believe it is possible for virtually every youngster to learn to read with fluency and to become successful in communicating ideas through writing, and, moreover, that nearly everyone can and should also reach levels of competence far beyond the daily demands for reading and writing that now inundate society. And I believe we learn to read primarily through practice, rather than by analysis.

The audience I have in mind as I have put these words down is anyone who desires to question the status quo, who wants to see an argument laid out, who takes the rationalist position in problem solving, who is interested in finding the bases for change. Some of that audience consists of teachers and teachers-to-be, along with others who make their living working in school settings, all students themselves in one way or another. Others are those parents particularly intent upon creating the kind of environment that will facilitate the language abilities of their children and who want to be in control of the decisions they make in that regard. Finally, there are those who are simply curious about this strange phenomenon we call "reading."

LEARNING TO READ

The Quest for Meaning

CHAPTER 1

The Problem of Literacy

"Reading," as one 5-year-old put it, "is telling stories in your head." In the pages that follow we will see just how apt a definition that is, one so deceptively simple that only a child could come up with it. Reading is in fact an extraordinarily complex process that is still not well understood, despite the decades spent on research analyzing various aspects of what we have traditionally perceived reading to be. Each year the *Reading Research Quarterly* publishes a list, with précis, of what the editors consider the most important studies in the field of reading in a given year; space constraints currently limit these lists to about a thousand such reports annually. The number of studies relating to reading has been increasing with each year; the overall total now runs to the tens of thousands.

In the chapters that follow, we will explore the many facets of reading behavior and draw inferences that will help us construct a coherent view of the reading process. Once such a perspective is established, ideas should emerge to guide our own behavior as adults who strive to help children acquire this ability so urgently desired in American society.

There is, I believe, something unique about the American focus on literacy. It derives from our heritage, with its firmly rooted belief that literacy is fundamental to both individual development and the national good. As a result, we see universal literacy as not only desirable but vital, and our inability to achieve that goal has been a continuing source of frustration.

The demand for universal literacy arrived on the shores of Massachusetts with the Pilgrims in 1620. The religious beliefs of these first settlers required that each person be able to read the Bible with sufficient understanding to obviate the need for a priesthood to stand between the individual and his or her God in comprehending good and evil. In the first few years of colonization, it was expected that fathers would teach their children, most importantly their sons, to read. However, it became evident early on that such teaching was not being performed satisfactorily, and in 1647 — hardly 25 years after the first successful attempt at settlement by Europeans — the colonists passed "Ye Olde Deluder Satan Act" in an effort to remedy this deficiency. The act called for the establishment in each community of a school where the children, both boys and girls, would be taught to read and write by a literate person, usually a woman. The genius of the act lay in the taxing authority contained in it, for out of this legislation was to emerge a unique institution, the American free public school system.

The singular objective of those early schools soon gave way to multiple objectives as the colonies coalesced into a nation and as nationhood led from a rural agricultural society into the complexities of modern living we know today. But basic to each development along the way has been the thrust toward universal literacy begun during the Colonial period. It has been assumed that literacy for all is fundamental both to individual realization in a society growing increasingly complex and to the survival of the democratic ideal.

What *Is* Literacy?

Before going any further, it is important to point out that getting a fix on exactly what constitutes "literacy" is difficult. Our measuring stick necessarily has to be more like a rubber band than a precise rule that gives the same answer each time we use it. Societal and cultural factors interact with problems inherent in measuring a phenomenon such as reading over time. Usually we think of literacy not only as demonstrating competence in reading and writing but also as being able to manipulate the number system with reasonable accuracy. A strict dictionary definition refers, however, only to competence in reading and writing. But how does one define competence? While that will depend upon a variety of things, the definition arises principally from what is expected by a particular society, or by a culture within it. Those expectations are subject to such diverse variables as the technological level of a society and the value system (or systems) represented within it. For example, consider how the interplay of these factors would lead Senegal, Western Europe, and India each to define "literacy" at a different level of competence.

But in addition to these rather broad measures of difference, there is the question of a more precise definition. How does one measure "reading" and "writing"? Some of the finer points in this measurement problem will be discussed more fully in a later chapter. Suffice it here to point out that our measures are at best imprecise and at worst off the mark, focusing on elements that may have little or nothing to do with the quality of either reading or writing. Add to that the difficulty in getting a fix on change in the literacy scene over time. For one thing, any meaningful length of time — say a generation of 20 or so years — leaves us with research results based on the administration of different tests, or measures of competence, and thus with data that are not directly comparable. Moreover, the test scores we do have report results from different populations: We test two groups of individuals and then "compare" results that are not really comparable because the subjects are not the same. Little wonder that pronouncements about the extent of the literacy problem vary widely (see Kozol, 1985). Two articles do provide helpful discussions of the nature and extent of the term *literacy* (see Bormuth, 1973–1974; Clifford, 1984). In a more recent study, Stedman and Kaestle (1987) attempt to compare past performance on various measures, including standardized tests. While admitting that "then-and-now studies are methodologically weak," the authors report that

> students' reading performance at a given age remained stable until the 1970s. The test decline that then occurred was not as great as many educators think, and much of it can be explained by the changing demographics of test-takers. The decline pales when compared to the tremendous increase in the population's educational attainment over the past 40 years. However, the strategy of ever-increasing schooling to meet ever-increasing literacy demands may have run its course. High school dropout rates are increasing, and educational attainment has leveled off. . . . In spite of their flaws, functional literacy tests suggest that 20% of the adult population, or 30 million people, have serious difficulties with common reading tasks. (p. 8)

To clarify the issue of what constitutes the acquisition of literate behavior, there have been attempts to identify different levels of achievement in this regard. One term in current use is "functional literacy," defined as the level of competence that allows an individual to make reasonable use of the resources available within a society — to balance a checkbook, read labels and follow directions, discern ambiguities in information, and write sufficiently well to communicate simple ideas — and to succeed in such tasks as filling out employment papers and applications for drivers' licenses, loans, and so forth. While this certainly is not literacy in its fullest flower, it is apparently a level not yet attained by a significant number of individuals in American society. Some parts of that society — particularly but not exclusively the black community, the Hispanic community, and some of the other ethnic minorities — fall farther short of the goal than do others. Although such information is

undoubtedly important, our measures of the extent of "functional literacy," or more accurately, its lack, do not provide us with data of any
exactitude.

We will not worry the bone of precisely how many are or are not
"literate," and inferentially who is or is not capable enough in their use
of language to qualify for a particular appellation. What we know with
sufficient certainty to warrant concern is that the problem of literacy is
widespread, and particularly that it affects important segments of the
society more grievously than others. Jonathan Kozol (1985) has done a
useful service, I think, in his analysis of the problem. In *Illiterate
America*, after reviewing the pratfalls in official estimates of the literacy
problem (he judges their findings to be far too optimistic), he suggests
that estimates showing it to be around 84 million adults are not far off
the mark. He quotes from a study done at the University of Texas in 1973
which concludes that "30 million men and women are now 'functionally
incompetent'" while "another 54 million 'just get by'"(p. 9). Kozol, for
his part, estimates that in 1984 there were 25 million adults who could
not "understand the antidote instructions on a bottle of corrosive kitch-
en lye," and that an additional 35 million were not competent enough to
understand instructions on a federal income tax return. In Kozol's view,
"all of these 60 million people should be called 'illiterate in terms of U.S.
print communication,'" or of the estimated 174 million in the adult
population of the United States, over one-third are unable to read and
write well enough to take advantage of the opportunities available in
American society (p. 10). It is worth noting that Kozol does not indicate
any faith that the schools are capable of remedying the situation. Instead, he calls for a massive literacy campaign by the adult community,
not unlike that which has transformed the literacy situation, if not the
politics, of countries such as Cuba and Nicaragua in recent years.

A Brief History of American Reading Instruction

Obviously, we are experiencing a great deal of turmoil in our quest
for the goal of universal literacy. During the two hundred years following the passage of "Ye Olde Deluder Satan," it was generally assumed
that failure to learn to read or write was an individual problem. If a
youngster was unable to benefit from the instruction, it was not the
fault of the teacher but of the student. Reading was taught during that
period much as it had been for centuries. For example, an Athenian,
writing in about 20 B.C., described the process: "When we are taught to
read, first we learn off the names of the letters, then their forms and

their values, then in due course syllables and their modifications, and finally words and their properties" (Mathews, 1966, p. 6).

Until the 1840s, that was essentially the way American children were expected to learn to read. At first, they were taught using something called a Hornbook, a small paddle-like board on which the alphabet appeared, perhaps with some common blends (i.e., "th," "fr," etc.), a short prayer, and a cross. The Hornbook actually was named for the sheet of horn — the forerunner of transparent plastics — that covered the letters to prevent dirty little hands from smudging them. Many children got no farther than recognizing the cross. In fact it is from this symbol that the saying "mark your X" comes, since if one failed to learn to write his or her name, a personal rendition of the cross could be used for a signature. Books gradually replaced the Hornbook, but success fell far short of expectations. It gradually became evident that the failure to learn to read and write was not necessarily entirely the fault of the individual. Some, like Horace Mann (1796–1859), began to decry inappropriate teaching methods as a primary source for the failure of children to learn the things it was intended schools would teach.

The Whole-Word vs. Phonics Controversy

Mann had become the Secretary to the Massachusetts School Board, a new position, in 1837. Barely a third of the children in the state were attending school, actually a fairly high percentage when compared with the other states. Those who did attend counted their time in class in weeks rather than in months, and teachers themselves frequently were unable to do simple multiplication and division problems. The distinguished historian, Merle Curti (1959), has written that the year Mann took office, some three hundred teachers were driven from their schools by pupils who no longer would suffer their cruelties.

In 1844 Mann and his wife, Mary Peabody, traveled to Europe to learn how the Europeans were dealing with the problem of education, a pilgrimage that intellectuals in all areas of endeavor were to make during the nineteenth century. It was in Prussia that he discovered two things that were to have a profound influence on American education. The first was the organizational structure that is now so familiar to us: the graded, self-contained elementary school directed by a strong administrator. The efficiency of this arrangement struck him forcefully, and he was to bring the idea home and implant it in the schools. He also made another discovery, that of what we now call the "whole-word method" of teaching children to read — Mann called it simply the "word method" (Mathews, 1966).

Mann believed that the word method held the promise of solving the literacy problem that permeated the schools of the day, and, with the help of his articulate wife, he proceeded to use his influence to install it in the Boston schools under his jurisdiction. Then, as now, nothing was entirely new under the sun, and Mann's "discovery," it turns out, had already been imported in somewhat altered form a decade or so before. Vociferous opposition to the "new method" soon appeared, not surprisingly led by the Boston schoolmasters, or school principals. So was born a controversy that has swirled about the educational scene with varying degrees of intensity ever since.

Whether the "whole-word method" has ever been a true alternative to a phonics-based methodology is a matter we will take up in detail in the next chapter. What we should realize here is that these two ways of conceptualizing the teaching of reading are not the only options open to us, and that they do not necessarily represent an appropriate response to the question of how children seem to learn to read. I use the word "seem" here advisedly because, as I have already noted and will continue to emphasize, despite assurances from many professional quarters to the contrary, we still know relatively little about how children learn to read, or write, or in fact to use language in any of its forms. What we do know is that language is a peculiarly human proclivity. Virtually everyone with an intact central nervous system develops the ability to use language; the exceptions to that assertion are indeed rare as a percentage of the general population. Does it follow, then, that we should as well have a relatively few number of problems with reading, and perhaps even writing, "all other things being equal"? As we shall see, there is a considerable differential among societies in the extent of the reading problem, with the United States experiencing a rate several times that of other countries that perceive universal literacy as an achievable national objective. Surely there must be reasons for this state of affairs.

An Alternative to Traditional Methods

The one clear alternative to the traditional approach to the teaching of reading is in itself not new, having its origins in the post–Civil War period, when the modern elementary school came into being. We shall call it a *naturalistic* or *experiential* approach to reading (and writing, as it turns out), contrasting it with what we might call a *subject-matter* approach, which is appropriately descriptive of both whole-word and phonics teaching methods. In the newer approach, the emphasis is on process, while in the earlier, it is upon developing awareness or knowledge about the behaviors and skills we associate with reading performance.

Just as there are variations between and within whole-word and phonics methods of teaching, the experiential approach has numerous variations. The unifying idea differentiating it from methods that assume one learns to read by learning about reading is, contrariwise, that reading is a process learned primarily through practice — one learns to read by reading, not by studying reading. Because of the longstanding traditional view that education consists primarily of instruction or direct teaching of specific information, the idea that one learns to read by reading, by experiencing reading directly, has never been widely accepted.

The theoretical base for the naturalistic view had its genesis in the progressivism and intellectual ferment that emerged in American thought during the latter third of the nineteenth century. A great deal of experimentation in education characterized that period, growing out of a profound belief in the school as a vehicle for individual and social improvement. The notion was widely accepted that "science" could provide a significant source for future betterment. So it was during this period that we saw the beginnings of the fields of education and psychology, from which systematic ideas about thinking and learning began their development.

Building a Psychology of Reading

Over these years, there were many false starts (e.g., attempts to specify "Laws of Learning"), and many downright errors in thinking (see Gould, 1981, for a remarkable history of the failed effort to assess human intelligence). However, the systematic study of human behavior, which commenced during this period, has, as we shall see, gradually provided a valuable data base from which we can more intelligently judge the alternatives we know to be available to us in our teaching.

The first comprehensive rationale for an experiential approach to the teaching of reading appeared in 1908 in a book by Edmund Burke Huey titled *The Psychology and Pedagogy of Reading*. Huey had been a student of G. Stanley Hall who, with William James, had in the 1880s and 1890s established psychology as an academic field in America. Huey spoke of the learning-to-read process as a natural one, best fostered in the parent's reading to the child:

> So, almost as naturally as the sun shines, in these sittings on the parents' knee, he comes to feel and to say the right parts of the story or rhyme as his

eye and finger travel over the printed lines, and all the earlier and more
certainly if illustrative pictures are placed hard by to serve as landmarks.
    The secret of it all lies in parents' reading aloud to and with the child.
(p. 10)

Huey believed, along with John Dewey and many others, that the
early years should be devoted primarily to the generation of ideas—
learning to think through direct experiencing (e.g., see Furth, 1970/
1986). If children did not become fluent readers in the home environment, then there was time enough to learn in a school environment
which replicated that of the home; in any event, Huey did not believe
formal instruction before the age of 9 or 10 was appropriate.
    Meanwhile, traditional notions of how children, or anyone else for
that matter, should be taught to read began to garner their own psychological, or "scientific," justification. While phonics began to lose support, both it and the newer whole-word method looked to the same
general root, what we have come to call the concept of *associationism:*
that learning results from developing an S-R bond, an association between a stimulus and an appropriate response. The assumption was
then, and remains in what we now refer to as behavioral psychology,
that the problem in all learning, and here particularly in learning to
read print, is primarily one of learning to associate a sound with its
appropriate symbol (or symbols, since in some instances different combinations of vowels and/or consonants represent the same sound, or
English phoneme). The so-called stimulus-response paradigm continues
to dominate our thinking, mainly because it reflects what has generally
been accepted as the way people learn things. If we go back to our
Athenian friends, they were clearly being taught with a crude form of S-
R methodology. How nice to have the conventional wisdom confirmed
with "scientific" evidence!
    The primitive phonics instruction of Athens extended, as we have
seen, well into the nineteenth century. If we think a bit more deeply
about it, the methodology that Horace Mann (and others) brought back
from Prussia was also based on the S-R idea. The difference between the
whole-word and phonics methods lies not in an abandonment of the
theory about how people learn to read, but instead in what should be
taught. In a phonics method, one teaches, and presumably learns, individual letter sounds (or the letters that blend into one sound), the individual phonemes of the language. From this "data base" the would-be
reader combines his knowledge of sound-symbol relationships into larger units, eventually into words that are recognized as meaningful. In a
whole-word methodology, the learner associates a group of letters (i.e.,

words) with the combination of sounds the entire word makes. After building up a repertoire of associations into what is termed a basic sight vocabulary, instruction then turns to finding words within individual words, and sounds within words, which can then be recombined into "new" words. Reading specialists speak of phonics as a "synthetic" methodology because the learner is expected to synthesize individual sounds into wholes. Whole-word methods are said to be "analytic" because they require the learner to analyze wholes into constituent parts which are then recombined into new words. Both methods are similar in their approach to the task of learning, however, because they both rely on developing an appropriate link between a stimulus and the response the learner makes to it.

We have been slow to recognize that for all practical purposes there is very little difference between the learning tasks we present to children when we choose a phonics or a whole-word method of teaching. We have instead expended tremendous amounts of energy arguing the superiority of one over the other. The schoolmasters of Boston had what can only be described as a conniption over Mann's proposals to abandon phonics for whole words in teaching. They and their intellectual descendants gradually lost out, however. Mann's argument for the "word method" was based on what was then a popular notion, an inheritance from the Enlightenment that swept Europe during the eighteenth century, namely, that we should make learning conform with the natural, what occurred in nature. Rousseau was the most articulate exponent of that view (see his *Emile*, 1762/1911). Clearly (or perhaps now not so clearly), words were more natural units to select for teaching than individual letter sounds. This view was gradually to gain professional support in the United States. Following the notion of a more "natural" unit in teaching, there was also both a "sentence" and a "paragraph" method, but these variants gained little popularity in the United States.

With the turn of the century, faith in science as the solution to all sorts of problems abounded, encompassing educational issues along with nearly everything else. Then, as now, there was great concern over the apparent failure of the schools to teach children to read. S-R psychology became a handy instrument for studying the problem because it emphasized analysis of elements of behavior which, it was believed, could be viewed directly. As with phonics, the problem of whole-word instruction was perceived as finding the most efficient way to teach children to give appropriate oral responses to certain kinds of visual stimulation behavior. The generation of meaning, or thinking, followed the establishment of the correct sound-symbol correspondences. This remains a widely held view of the problem facing a person who is learning to read.

The scientific study of reading thus early on took up a life of its own. Thinking was seen as the result of certain behaviors that were prerequisite to its generation. One could, therefore, "read" (i.e., go through all the steps of reading) literally without thinking. One could read a page, or whatever, without generating any useful ideas whatsoever. The teaching of reading was perceived not only as a subject in the school curriculum with a body of knowledge to be taught, but moreover as something clearly separated from other language activity. We learned to speak of "reading and the language arts." We taught reading behavior separately from everything else, divorcing it from writing (and as well divorcing writing from the mechanical formation of letters). We began to work on the notion of hierarchies of difficulty, of which words were "harder" to learn, of what skills should be taught and in which order instruction should proceed, and so forth—all along assuming that instruction, to be successful, should take each child along the same path.

The nadir of phonics instruction was brought nearer with the birth in 1930 of Dick and Jane in the first "basal reader textbooks," the Elson Readers. Co-authored by William Elson and William S. Gray (nicknamed "Mr. Reading" in the United States for over forty years), these textbooks laid claim to the scientific heritage which Gray, particularly, represented. Textbooks in reading had, of course, been published for many years, and "series" of sorts had been available since the mid-1800s—among them McGuffey's famous readers. The "modern" textbook, the forerunner of what we see today in most classrooms, is usually dated from the Elson readers, when it was first seriously claimed that the text was based on "scientific" knowledge of the learning process.

The Elson-Gray textbooks represented the first coordinated effort to provide an articulated series of readers based on a whole-word methodology. The appeal to scientism, and the ever attractive notion that the problem of reading could be solved through the selection of instructional materials, led this series to become a financial bonanza. Although virtually every major publisher of school texts would, over the next thirty or so years, bring out its version of these texts based on the assumptions of a whole-word methodology, Dick and Jane and their always clean, ordered, and simple world were the archetypal guides to the then growing number of persons devoting their professional skills to the problem of reading.

Phonics advocates thus were forced into a kind of underground. Eschewed as an appropriate method for "normal" children, phonics found a home where children with moderate to severe reading problems were concerned. It was, then, a kind of court of last resort until the mid-

1960s when Jean Chall published a book called *Learning to Read: The Great Debate* (1967/1983a). Chall undertook an analysis of trends in the development of the Dick and Jane readers and their imitators; combining this analysis with her own rationale about how children learn to read, she announced that she did not like what she saw. Following a "scientific rationale," Chall maintained that her review of research

> from 1912 to 1965 indicates that a code-emphasis method—i.e., one that views beginning reading as essentially different from mature reading and emphasizes learning of the printed code for the spoken language—produces better results, at least up to the point where sufficient evidence seems to be available, the end of the third grade. (p. 307)

Saying that a majority of American youngsters conform to this research (although not specifying the size of that majority), she urged adoption of what she termed a *code-emphasis* (or phonics) methodology over the "meaning-emphasis" approach Gray and others had sold so effectively as the successful method for teaching children to read.

Noting that "there are definite signs . . . that more children are now learning by a code-emphasis method than in the early 1960s" (p. 307), Chall reopened the doors of respectability to instruction approached with a phonics-oriented strategy. What had not changed, though, was that the "cure" for any reading problem continued to be seen as residing in the thing selected to do the teaching, namely, the textbook.

Since then, although publishers have once again felt there was a sufficient market to produce "code-emphasis" or phonics-oriented instructional materials, the predominant "method of choice" has remained, to use Chall's nomenclature, a "meaning-emphasis," or whole-word methodology. The feeling continues that the instructional package—that is, the textbook and such supplemental materials as workbooks, audiotapes, or other reinforcing instructional devices—remains a critically important element in the reading curriculum. Dominant practice still isolates reading instruction from other curriculum or teaching concerns, such as the teaching of computational skills, the science and social studies curriculums, the arts, and even writing.

When Huey and others introduced a naturalistic approach as an alternative to the traditional subject matter approach to the teaching of reading, toward the end of the nineteenth century, not surprisingly, relatively few teachers found themselves able to abandon traditional ways. While Huey's approach might make a certain kind of sense—particularly if one sees reading behavior as an extension of oral language, which is obviously learned with little if any formal instruction—

most teachers feared losing control of their teaching. The majority of
reading teachers still find their textbooks to be the proverbial classroom
security blanket, as do their administrators, who generally seek to keep
control over their schools much as individual teachers do over their
classrooms. The textbook is perceived to be the constant in a situation
that otherwise is full of unpredictable variables.

There have always been teachers who have marched to a different
drummer, of course, and so a small minority have over the years utilized
various techniques rooted in Huey's naturalistic approach. Thus there is
a continuing supporting "literature" in the fields of education and psychology; however, the majority of it was necessarily based on testimonial — not an insignificant argument where teachers are concerned, but a
poor competitor against data, observation, and "fact." As we shall see,
during the last 25 or so years, the experiential or naturalist approach has
gained substantive support from new research that lends a more direct
understanding of language-learning processes and from knowledge,
new to most teachers in the United States, about how thinking develops
in children. That data base has continued to expand. Although the
politics of American reading instruction has continued to militate
against teachers going outside of traditional methodologies, even
though they may secretly desire to do so, other factors are now beginning to erode that resistance. Principal among these is the widespread
public frustration over the evident failure of the schools to educate our
school-age population to satisfactory levels of literacy. That frustration
is being exacerbated, I believe, by the widespread publication of standardized test scores; despite occasional bits of evidence suggesting the
situation has perhaps improved, or at least stabilized, the scores have
generally been poor enough to cause a nationwide feeling of depression.
An associated aspect has been the emergence of a professional, and even
public, awareness that writing and reading are interrelated activities
that are dependent upon the presence of skill but are more fundamentally grounded in meaning. We consequently now see stirring a growing
interest in and awareness of those ways of teaching grounded in meaning rather than skill. It is, however, a relatively meager beginning if we
consider the tens of thousands of classrooms that together constitute the
public and private schools of the United States.

Reading in International Perspective

It comes as a surprise to most Americans that reading is not viewed
with anywhere near the alarm or concern — indeed, is not even seen as a
problem — in many other countries. World illiteracy is, of course, a most

serious and vexing problem, one which we ignore at our peril; it is estimated that about three-fourths of the world's population is illiterate. This means that over three billion of the earth's people can neither read nor write. And while the world's illiteracy rate (the percentage of the total world population of approximately 5 billion individuals who are illiterate) is declining, albeit slowly, the actual number of illiterate people is growing worldwide, simply because efforts to bring literacy skills into existence are being outstripped by an exploding birth rate.

But our attention here is focused on those countries where literacy is viewed as an achievable national goal. And here we find the discrepancy to which I have referred. None of those countries equals the United States in the percentage of children who experience problems in the beginning stages of learning or in the incidence of problems in the young-adult and adult populations. Several explanations for this discrepancy are commonly offered. The one heard most often is that English, particularly in its written (or printed) form, is a perverse animal, an arrangement of unexplainable exceptions that all too often defy logical analysis; in contrast, we are told, most other languages are "phonetically regular," possessing few of the arbitrary attributes of English, and are, therefore, available to logical deduction and consequently much easier to learn. Other explanations are that children in other societies are more docile and therefore more amenable to instruction, and that values in less heterogeneous societies encourage greater levels of success.

While there are doubtless grains of truth in these and a number of other arguments that will be discussed later, the fact remains that even among countries where English is the first or native language, the discrepancy persists. In England, for example, the estimate is that between 3% and 5% can appropriately be termed "backward readers" (see Bryant & Bradley, 1985; Ridgers, 1983; Yule et al., 1974). And in the Scandinavian countries, initial problems in learning to read print are encountered by about 5% of the children. This number is reduced to about 1% by the time children reach the age of 10 or so (Douglass, 1969). While the story of reading problems varies from one country to another, the fact remains that the difficulties encountered in the United States are simply not repeated at the same level of incidence in those countries where universal literacy is on the national agenda.

Of course, as we have seen, the definition of literacy varies from one country to another. Even given those variations, however, what we see in the United States is a much higher presence, both of initial difficulty in achieving fluency in reading behavior and of crippling inabilities to read (i.e., to read well enough to function with reasonable fullness in society). So marked is this difference between the American experience and that of England, Norway, Germany, and so forth, that it is surprising for educators in those countries to learn how much time we spend on formal instruction in reading. No other country, in fact, devotes as much instructional time to the teaching of reading, largely because of the early and widespread achievement of sufficient fluency and the consequent early utilitarian role reading ability comes to play in the curriculum. That is, although the schools in other countries may be more formal, structured, and even rigid and elitist than our own, children early on become sufficiently proficient in using reading as a vehicle for learning in the content areas. Thus, they polish their skills through reading in the areas of literature, history, geography, and science; in the process, even by inadvertence, they learn to read by reading. These observations derive mainly from my own experience studying schools in Norway, Denmark, England, Scotland, Korea, and the USSR, and through graduate students with whom I have worked over the years, particularly those from Africa and Asia.

Meanwhile in the United States, in typical American fashion, we launch a frontal attack on the problem by increasing the amount of time we devote to instruction. Goodlad (1984) and his associates have recently confirmed what has been known for a long time: that the largest portion of the school day goes to instruction in reading and the development of computational skills. They found, for example, that about 50% of a school week, by teacher report of time spent, was devoted to reading/language arts instruction in the early elementary grades, and about 45% of it in the upper grades; this obviously means that very close to half of every school day goes toward instruction in reading and the mechanics of spelling and writing (Sirotnik, 1983). Whether the method of teacher report reveals reality is a bit difficult to tell. From my own experience the time reported is likely to be low. Teachers have in recent years reduced the amount of time teaching art, music, drama, dance, and even science and social studies, and they would in the main be reluctant to report no attention to these areas, even were that the case; the areas getting the lion's share of attention therefore might well be underreported. In any case, our elementary schools have largely become literacy schools, yet the payoff for that emphasis is difficult to see.

In our secondary schools, too, there is growing attention to the problem of reading. Virtually every intermediate or junior high school and high school has classes devoted to the formal teaching of reading. Such programs are often extensive. Today it is the exceptional post-secondary institution that does not field classes, often given for academic credit, that focus on the development of reading skills. Admittedly, some of these are geared to relatively advanced work, but everyone in the educational establishment is fully aware that there are many students in our colleges and universities seriously deficient in their reading abilities (and, I must add, in writing, a matter which is being addressed through a new, nationwide network of writing centers). Some will argue that this is a new phenomenon and, particularly on our West and East coasts, attributable in large part to the recent influx of immigrants, especially from Central and South America and Asia. No doubt the situation has been exacerbated by this development; however, it cannot hide the reality of the large number of indigenous students who are not sufficiently literate to survive academic life without special assistance, and whose survival even then is in very fragile condition.

Beyond Functional Literacy

There is a good chance, then, that we have largely brought the literacy problem down upon ourselves. Locked in the arms of behavioral psychology, we have misread the nature of the beast we wish to tame. We have failed to perceive, it seems to me, that reading is a generic form of behavior that will emerge if we will only let it. It is, I think, presumptuous for us to assume that this activity can be taught didactically. As Hodges and Rudorf pointed out several years ago, when summarizing what they believe teachers should know about the similarities between language acquisition and reading acquisition: "It is only in a trivial sense that we can teach a child to read, any more than we can teach him to speak" (1972, p. 227).

This is not to say that teaching is irrelevant for the child who, like all other children, very much wants to learn to read print. We know there is a tremendous inner motivation in American children to become literate, and it is inconceivable that we can ignore the questions that arise from that interest. Can the children's not realizing that drive really be the result of some inherent individual lack or personal failure? Teaching is crucial if we are to have a truly literate society. The question is, however, what kind of teaching provides the greatest chance for success in that endeavor? Teaching designed to *invoke* reading behavior has, it is clear, failed us. But reading can be *evoked* very easily, and that is the kind of teaching I will describe in the pages that follow.

As we move into that discussion, I would ask that the reader be open to a view of reading other than that of a subject best learned through the study and practice of its component skills: that of a process best learned through the practice or "doing" of reading.

But, you may well ask, is it not possible to accommodate the subject-matter/process dichotomy? Is it not really a compatible dyad instead of a mutually exclusive one? Because teachers often feel they lack sufficient specific information about how children learn, there is always a tendency to try to combine competing ideas into an eclectic melange that, it is hoped, "covers all the bases." This tendency is particularly strong where the potential for failure is present. Although we know that a few children learn to read spontaneously, with a minimum of assistance, it is extremely difficult to consider such behavior as a harbinger of all development. We cling instead to the notion that learning to read ultimately occurs almost exclusively from being within a controlled environment, even though the idea of development through practice is an attractive one. However, it remains that cause and effect in teaching and learning are as hard to establish when teaching takes place within a didactic frame as they are when learning occurs primarily through practice.

As we shall see, however reading comes about, it cannot be observed directly. We can only infer from indirect evidence that the desired behavior has taken place. For this reason we are denied direct knowledge of whether something we intended to implant — namely, the ability to create meanings for print that are truly comprehensible to the child — actually came into existence as a direct result of our teaching. It consequently behooves us to maintain an open mind regarding cause and effect, to suspend our rush to judgment regarding the role of formal instruction in the learning-to-read process.

In the pages that follow, the theories lying behind behavioral and naturalistic or experiential conceptions of reading and the teaching of reading are presented for the reader's evaluation. And whether they can exist side by side or are indeed largely mutually exclusive will, I believe, become clearer in the reader's mind. If the problem of reading is to have any solution, it is in any event important to avoid conclusions reached by way of an uninformed belief system. As we shall also see, there is a wealth of new knowledge available to consider as we approach the problem of reading, knowledge that now allows a more rational consideration of the issues than has hitherto been available to the profession.

Related Readings

Balmuth, M. (1989). *The roots of phonics: A historical introduction.* New York: Teachers College Press. (Original work published 1982)

Bormuth, J. R. (1978). Value and volume of literacy. *Visible Language, 12,* 118–161.

Clifford, G. J. (1984). *Buch und lesen:* Historical perspectives on literacy and schooling. *Review of Educational Research, 54,* 472–500.

Cook, W. D. (1977). *Adult literacy education in the United States.* Newark, DE: International Reading Association.

Dillon, D. A. (1981). Literacy and mainstream culture in American history. *Language Arts, 58,* 207–218.

Farb, P. (1974). *Word play: What happens when people talk.* New York: Knopf.

Fisher, D. L. (1981). Functional literacy tests: A model of question-answering and an analysis of errors. *Reading Research Quarterly, 16,* 418–448.

Guthrie, J. T. (1981). Reading in New Zealand: Achievement and volume. *Reading Research Quarterly, 17,* 6–27.

Imamura, A. E. (1986). Back to basics: The family and the school in Japan. *Issues in Education, 14,* 52–64.

Jansen, M., et al. (1978). *The teaching of reading — without really any method: An analysis of reading instruction in Denmark.* New York: Humanities Press.

Johnson, D. D. (1973–1974). Sex differences in reading across cultures. *Reading Research Quarterly, 9,* 67–86.

Kirsch, I., & Guthrie, J. T. (1977–1978). The concept and measurement of functional literacy. *Reading Research Quarterly, 13,* 485–507.

Kozol, J. (1978). A new look at the literacy campaign in Cuba. *Harvard Educational Review, 48,* 341–377.

Martuza, V. (Ed.). (1981). Education in Cuba: 1961–1981 (special issue commemorating the 20th anniversary of Cuba's National Literacy Campaign). *Journal of Reading, 25.*

McCall, C. (1987). Women and literacy: The Cuban experience. *Journal of Reading, 30,* 318–325.

Ollila, L. O. (Ed.). (1981). *Beginning reading instruction in different countries.* Newark, DE: International Reading Association.

O'Neil, W. (1970). Properly literate. *Harvard Educational Review, 40,* 260–263.

Resnick, D. P., & Resnick, L. B. (1977). The nature of literacy: An historical exploration. *Harvard Educational Review, 47,* 370–385.

Robinson, H. A. (1977). *Reading and writing instruction in the United States: Historical trends.* Newark, DE: International Reading Association and ERIC Clearinghouse on Reading & Communication Skills.

Smith, F. (1983). *Essays into literacy.* Portsmouth, NH: Heinemann Educational Books.

Truer, A. W. (1896). *History of the horn-book.* 2 vols. London: Leadenhall.

Ylisto, I. P. (1977). Early reading responses of young Finnish children. *The Reading Teacher, 30,* 167–172.

CHAPTER 2

Reading Reading

What are we talking about when we speak of *reading*? What do humans do when they read print? It has been a rare event, indeed, when any extended consideration is given to the nature of reading behavior. For example, William S. Gray, mentioned in the previous chapter and long the most revered and respected figure in the field of reading in the United States, defined it in his widely read book, *On Their Own in Reading* (1948/1960), in what amounted to little more than a side comment: "In order to read — to receive ideas from printed language — a child must associate sound and meaning with printed words" (p. 9). More a description than a definition, actually. And like most writers then and since, he did not return to the problem of definition again, preferring to get along with what is still generally perceived to be the main problem of the pedagogue, namely, to identify what ought to be taught so that "reading" might occur. To take a reading on reading required no more than that.

So as we turn the leaves of those who would tell us how reading should be taught, we have few guides to the ultimate nature of this behavior, and thus little rationale for any particular strategy to bring it into being. We are given a variety of very detailed maps for *teaching* reading, but no overview of the territory that "reading" itself comprehends. If we have only the dimmest of views of what might be thought to constitute reading behavior, how can we possibly feel sure that what we do as pedagogues, whether at home or at school, helps people learn to read?

"What is reading?" is consequently not a throw-away question, even though it has frequently been treated as such; it should be a central focus of anyone concerned with literacy, because the response we give to that question will determine how we proceed.

Reading and the Conventional Wisdom

The traditional view, more frequently unstated or implied than put directly, can be summarized in what has become the standard cliché, that "reading is getting meaning from the printed page." There are countless variations of that "definition," some simple, others complex. For example, in one of the more popular teacher education textbooks, a dozen different "definitions" from reading authorities are listed (see Dallman et al., 1960/1982, pp. 22–27). While the words vary, the basic idea expressed in nearly all of them revolves around the definition given by Frank Smith (1971): "Reading is an act of communication in which information is transferred from a transmitter to a receiver" (p. 12). Chall, like many others, omits any discussion of reading behavior per se in her recent book, *Stages of Reading Development* (1983b). Her overall view of the issues involved, however, is derived from the principle that learning to read precedes reading to learn. In Stage 1 (ages 6–7) of her scheme, for example, she describes the initial problem in learning to read as "learning the arbitrary set of letters and associating these with the corresponding parts of spoken words"(p. 16). In Stage 2 (ages 7–8) the reader consolidates what was learned in Stage 1. "Stage 2 is not for gaining new information, but for confirming what is already known to the reader," she writes (p. 18). Stage 3 marks the beginning of reading to learn: "When readers enter Stage 3, they start on the long course of reading to 'learn the new' — new knowledge, information, thoughts and experiences" (p. 20). Regardless of the rhetoric, what is generally meant, and believed, is that the foundation of all reading behavior rests upon establishing sound symbol "correspondences," that is, of associating sound(s) with symbol(s) so that meaning is derived, and that all subsequent reading rests on fluency in "decoding" — transforming that "arbitrary set of letters" into corresponding sounds, which are then recognized as meaningful. It is thus viewed as a linear activity: One begins with visual stimulation by means of print either through symbols representing single phonemes (à la phonics) or through groups of symbols representing whole words. It may be useful in this regard to recall the discussion in the previous chapter regarding the origins of the "whole-word vs. phonics controversy." In either case, visual stimulation provides the basis for developing an association with its corresponding auditory signal. Satisfactory (or correct) correspondence of sound with symbol leads to the generation of an auditory letter or word memory which brings about recognition of it as some kind of meaningful unit. In phonics-based instruction, "meaning" is reached through knowledge of letter sounds. In whole-word instruction, meaning is attained through knowledge of a word as an auditory component. In neither instance is what we might call true meaning absolutely essential. In the former instance, the ability to "say" the sound suffices ("ah" for *a*, for example); in the latter, the ability to "say" the word is the criterion for success. In the initial stages of the learning-to-read process, meaning in the sense of

comprehending, that is, of experiencing understanding, is relatively un-
important (and in the case of phonics-based instruction, of no central
significance).

Thus the conventional wisdom holds that reading acquisition is the
process of establishing correct sound-symbol correspondences, and all
instruction focuses on the successful establishment of these relationships. Teaching proceeds on the notion that while reading may be best
described as a global process, fluency is best established through direct
instruction of the various parts or skills that we observe exist within
successful readers. Reading is, as a result, taught as a subject in the
school curriculum.

Sources of the "Subject Matter" of Reading Instruction

But whence does the "subject" matter of reading derive? As I have
already noted, there are two generally accepted sources. The first is the
"code-emphasis," or phonics curriculum. It traditionally relies upon logical pedagogical analyses of word parts, that is, of the obvious phonetic
bases of, in the American case, English. One might expect agreement
about what parts of this phonemic data bank ought to be taught. No
such agreement exists, however. Ever since the invention of the textbook
in the early 1800s, one "system" has replaced another.

Instructional materials based on a phonics or "code emphasis" approach reflect to a very great extent the personal experiences of their
authors — who believe they have a unique methodology — and of their
postulants (many teachers embrace a particular method of instruction
with a religious fervor). As a consequence, particular methods of instruction are often marketed under the names of their "authors," or in
other cases, the "senior authors" are given much prominence in the
advertising literature. For a period, particularly during the 1960s and
1970s, when phonics-based instruction was regaining its respectability,
the linguistic scholar's influence in providing criteria for selecting the
subject matter for this instructional approach grew all out of propor-
tion. The acceptance of linguists into the house of reading derived from
the hope that this time-honored discipline would lend a scientific respectability to the rehabilitation of phonics-based instruction. It did
that, but rather fleetingly as it has turned out, for the linguists proved
no more capable than their teacher-turned-writer brethren in creating a
universal approach to teaching based on the synthetic principle of language instruction. The end result is a wide variety of schemes, each
introducing consonant and vowel sound patterns unique to each set of

materials. The common bond is the rather unusual personal loyalty which phonics-based programs generate.

Another source exists for selecting a "subject matter" in reading instruction where the whole-word method is concerned. Viewing reading from a behaviorist point of view — that is, from direct observations of behavior we commonly associate with this activity — the whole-word advocate articulates a series of skills derived from the analysis of mature reading behavior. It is assumed that these "behaviors," when taught individually and in a "developmental sequence," will result in fluent or "mature" reading performance that will mirror the model from which they were derived. As in a phonics-based reading curriculum, the whole is presumed to be the sum of its parts; only in defining the parts is there disagreement as to the nature of the problem of reading.

Not surprisingly, whole-word advocates have as much, or more, difficulty in deciding what is significant in parsing the behavior of fluent readers. As a consequence, no two reader series, or "basal readers," are the same. Each defines its own repertoire of skills and the order in which they should be taught; each has its own "sight-word" vocabulary, and so on. Although the variability among textbook series has been known for a long time, even today the general impression is that any differences are relatively minor. John Hockett's 1938 study, for example, demonstrated the variability in vocabulary among books very early on, a matter he believed would aid in the development of reading skill (p. 32). The popular notion since has been that "vocabulary control" is essential to the development of reading ability, although commonalities in this regard are still not to be found either in vocabulary between series or in other fundamental aspects of these books. Chall (1983a) chronicles the results of attempts to cope with the issue of variability within the so-called basal reader textbook series, but the result has been more one of reducing the extent of the vocabulary, sentence length, and the like, rather than reaching any common agreement between different published series — a "dumbing-down" that is, I believe, difficult to justify.

The modern reader series, whether based on a whole-word or phonics approach, do, however, hold in common the importance of several teaching and learning principles. They assume, for example, that instructional processes require standardization. To that end, each provides an extensive "teacher's manual" that contains detailed suggestions for teacher instruction. Each also provides extended "workbook" activities that accompany the individual instructional lessons; children are expected to complete these lessons as a form of reinforcement for what has been taught in the instructional lesson.

Another very significant assumption underlying whole-word methods is that learning and teaching proceed most efficiently when children of the same general reading ability are grouped together. Most teacher's manuals presume there will be grouping within each classroom based on ability. Normally, that calls for three subgroupings, although all conscientious teachers will quickly point out that there will in every classroom always be three or four children who fall outside, and usually below, that range. Studies over the years have shown that children tend to be classified very early in their school careers with regard to their membership in these instructional subgroups (which often go under various euphemisms). Such membership tends to persist through the grades; where there is movement from one group to another, the chances of assignment downward are much greater than a change to a "higher" group (e.g., see Oakes, 1985, p. 51). In contrast to instruction in phonics, where letter sounds are primary, the significant unit of instruction in whole-word methodologies is the individual word. The principle of this so-called "analytic" method of instruction is, as I have pointed out, mastery of a "sight vocabulary" from which parts are taken to reconstruct "new" words. In early instruction, children are expected to associate the configuration of whole words with their sounds, which in turn is said to result in recognition of the word as a meaningful unit. But whole-word methods are not based purely on this kind of associationism. Very early on children are urged to "give the sound of the first (or last) letter," and to engage in other kinds of analyses that are based on phonics. (Similarly, phonics methodologies begin to employ analytic as well as synthetic techniques in their instruction as teaching progresses.) Nonetheless, the major emphasis is upon recognizing words as "wholes," and to that end reading textbooks based on this approach contain exercises designed to teach the "new words" appearing in each book in the series. The belief that recognizing isolated words is the backbone to success in fluent reading is so intense that individual words are often taught as such. And it is common practice for teachers (often at the behest of their administrator) to require children to demonstrate the ability to reproduce on command evidence they can "read" the words when they appear in list form. Of course, "saying" and "reading" may be two quite different things. And that brings forth again my concern with meaning in these kinds of instructional activities. Many children who experience difficulty in acquiring a sight vocabulary appear to be saying words (critics of phonics methods have called a similar difficulty "barking at print") with no apparent consciousness of meaning.

The Role of Meaning in Reading

As we have seen, traditional forms of reading instruction generally perceive the derivation of meaning in reading to be the result of developing an association or "correspondence" between a printed symbol and its auditory counterpart, or, as it is also said, of "decoding." Although authorities disagree over how one should teach this decoding process, they assume that certain skills are prerequisite to the derivation of meaning. A shared (and in my view equally inaccurate) assumption is that one literally "gets" meaning from print, that meanings somehow lie outside of the reader. During instruction, for example, we speak of words as having meanings quite apart from the personal experience of the reader. But consider the following:

Reflection makes it only too obvious that a word, whether in its oral, handwritten, or printed form, has no meaning in and of itself. In its oral form, language consists of a series of commonly understood auditory signals that are unique to a particular speech community. As we shall see, the earliest stages in learning to speak and to comprehend oral language are not dependent in any sense upon an awareness of words as individual entities. The young child perceives language holistically, both as it utters sounds and as it interprets them in communication. Even adults, in oral communication, pay little or no attention to the existence of lexical items, or words. Transcriptions of oral language are consequently quite different from much written language, especially that of well-honed prose or poetry, of legal or other technical jargons. So different are some of them that we sometimes hear arguments over whether they do not have entirely different roots!

Like oral language, written or printed language emerges from a particular language community. And like oral language, it possesses no inherent meaning. It is, at once simply and in all its complexity, nothing more or less than the result of the most basic of human proclivities, namely, the unique capacity to think symbolically and the inevitable need to engage in social concourse. Human societies, developing in widely diverse environments and with consequent differences in values, have evolved astonishingly diverse languages. Not surprisingly, their printed and written representations also differ drastically. Speakers of English and other European languages deal with the Roman alphabet arranged in horizontal rows proceeding from left to right and from top to bottom on a page, and from "front" to "back" of a book. But in Arabic, symbols emerge from right to left, and books are therefore paginated in what in English would be "back to front." Although English speakers are used to "words" appearing as such with a minimum of punctuation or representations of pronunciation, with meanings presented through different arrangements of the alphabet, some languages, like Vietnamese and Thai, appear to us as a complex series of superadded phonetic signs signaling differences in meaning among many "words" spelled the same. There are, of course, language families related by common (though often distant) roots, but across the entire spectrum of human language, the diversity is remarkable. That diversity and the evident ability of very different language communities to become "literate" suggests that relatively few problems in learning to read inhere in the print itself. It would suggest, rather, that most such problems lie elsewhere.

To put it another way, consider that we use language to express our ideas but that words are not ideas. This difference between what we know or think and the role of language is illustrated well, I believe, by the difficulties we all experience trying to communicate. If thoughts could be represented linguistically with any preciseness, there would be much less misunderstanding, and there would be much less need to use language. Once we had said, or written, we would not need to say or write more. Of course, we always need more rather than less language, for despite the extent of its vocabulary, its storage system for housing the concepts of a speech community, and no matter how carefully we arrange words to represent our ideas, language remains insufficient to the task. That holds true for the speaker or writer and, perhaps more vividly, for the listener or reader.

The problem for listener or speaker, or reader or writer, is, therefore, that meaning lies not "out there" but within our own experience. Symbols provide a convenient stimulus for bringing those ideas to the surface of awareness. Dewey (1938) spoke of learning as "the reconstruction of experience." What he meant is that we learn by making connections between new and past experiences such that novel ideas or meanings become available to us. Jean Piaget, the Swiss epistemologist/psychologist, spoke of learning as a process involving assimilation and accommodation in which experiencing is then accommodated by the learner into pre-existing patterns of knowing. The result of the assimilation/accommodation dyad is a continuous state he termed "equilibration." According to Piaget, the human organism is never in a completely static state; rather, it is constantly experiencing and constantly accommodating that experience, constantly growing and changing, "reconstructing." In this process, the organism is selective; it "accommodates" through the assimilative process that which can be fitted into past patterns of experience (Piaget & Inhelder, 1964; Piaget, 1985; Ginsburg & Opper, 1979).

Reading, or writing, like listening or speaking, provides an avenue for reconstructing experience, stimulating the equilibration process, and thus learning. Most importantly, according to this view, the *search for meaning* is what drives the organism to activity. We seek to *evoke* meanings through the only avenues we have available to us: the sense modalities, through sight, hearing, touch, taste, through our kinesthetic and gustatory awareness.

When writers write and readers read, then, words potentially represent a point of common contact, but each approaches the problem of writing and reading within the context of his or her own experience. For the writer, words represent his or her ideas. Strings of words, sentences if you will, are devised with some kind of audience in mind and are arranged accordingly. Readers approach the writer's text with only their experience to help them create the meanings that the reading suggests to them.

Toward a Definition:
Reading as a Naturalistic Activity

I have suggested that reading behavior is not directly observable. We can only infer that reading has taken place: We observe eyes move in the manner we associate with visual pursuit across the page, we see another person apparently intent on responding to print on a page, we inquire through our questions, we perhaps prepare and administer some kind of formal test to see if we can tell whether the response we observe appears to be associated with the tasks that were set before the reader. But the evidence of reading per se is available to us only after the fact. That is because all reading is an internalized kind of behavior that is silent in nature. Whatever sounds may be in evidence, as we shall see in a subsequent chapter, are present only as confirmatory for the reader, not as a precondition to reading itself. In considering this proposition, it may be useful to appreciate that when we refer to "oral reading" we are actually misnaming the activity we are trying to describe. It would be more accurately defined as "saying out loud that which has already been read," awkward as that phrasing may be. To test this assertion, I suggest reading something aloud, preferably to someone else, at a moderate rate that emphasizes meaning. Note that the eye tends to move ahead of the word being spoken; thus, for the fluent reader, at least, "reading" has already taken place when each word is "said." For the beginning reader, "look and say" more closely approximates what is going on. And many youngsters do seem to become stuck at this level, perhaps as a consequence of teaching that continues to focus on the sequential "saying" of individual words rather than on the meaning to be generated from the text.

Since reading, what we shall for the moment call "making meaning," occurs within the reader, print, or the "thing to be read," is peripheral to the process itself. By saying it is peripheral, I do not intend to imply that it is not significant. I mean to emphasize that the particular nature of the print, the stimulus, is not critical to the process. If its characteristics were critical, then we would necessarily find differences in the competence with which readers read the wide variety of systems that have been developed to represent language. That kind of difference we do not find. What we observe is that human beings in different cultural and other environmental circumstances have, as already noted, created a very wide range of symbol systems to represent their own particular speech community. While the Roman alphabet has facilitated that representation in numerous ways, it is still not the only manner in which languages can be represented. Thus is it that the particular form of the symbol system fails to be critical in the learning-to-read process.

The question then must be raised as to whether reading print, no matter its peculiar characteristic, is uniquely different from other perceptual processes we draw upon to create meanings. In everyday life we refer to the reading of many different kinds of things. We read faces as well as words, situations as well as numbers. If there is something unique about those symbols that represent the oral language of a speech community, what might that uniqueness consist of? It is generally agreed that blind persons who "read" Braille are indeed reading. How similar, or different, are the two processes? Are they essentially one, or are there fundamental differences between them?

I take the position that, while we can identify certain characteristics about print as it appears before us on the page, we must assume those characteristics are not fundamental either to fluent reading or, for that matter, to the initial stages of learning to read. I come to that conclusion not just because the print itself takes various forms, nor because the configuration we give our handwriting is quite different from that of print, nor because we must consider the reading of Braille as true reading, nor even because speech communities employ a wide variety of symbol systems to represent their oral language. Instead, I find it self-evident that symbols themselves possess no inherent meaning. Thus it is the meaning we give to the symbol that is of preeminent importance to the process.

In the chapters that follow I shall argue for a shift from "unlocking the code," which tends to dominate our thinking as the primary problem in the learning-to-read process, to meaning and the desire to create meanings, which is an inherent human drive. The fundamental behavior that parents or the teachers of reading must capture and help direct is the quest for meaning on which we are all embarked. Child and adult alike pursue this quest; sometimes this occurs in ways that others may not approve, but it is without question a drive basic to all human behavior. In this sense all our conscious hours are engaged in reading.

The position taken here, then, is that *reading is the process of creating meanings for any and every thing in the environment for which the reader develops an awareness.* In this sense we are engaged in the same kind of activity as reading print when we "create meanings" from auditory stimulation, be they spoken words or music. The same analogy may be drawn between reading and any other kind of sensory stimulation in which meaning results. Although what follows is an attempt to explicate this position particularly where print reading and writing are concerned, the entire argument depends upon viewing the issue of literacy from a broader vantage point. Reading print thus appears in a context in which different priorities are evident as we think of the teaching/learning dyad.

In 1917, E. L. Thorndike, in a seminal article, wrote of reading as reasoning. The parsimony of that assertion belies the complexity of the interaction, of course. One who developed this notion perhaps more than anyone else was Peter L. Spencer (1961), who argued that reading "is as native to human behavior as is digestion, respiration, or any other of the fundamental life processes" (pp. 3–4). He explained:

> There is no question but that printed words must be sensed, recognized, interpreted, and effectively dealt with if they are to serve the purpose for which they were produced. But, that is likewise the case for spoken words, gestures, and all other modes of expression which may be used in communication. The process of sensing, cognizing, and responding with regard for all such stimuli is basically the same. Hence, designating only one of these activities as reading-behavior is an arbitrary procedure. (1973, p. 206)

Spencer saw the development of reading behavior as an emergent process: "It begins with simple intuitive reactions and becomes special-

ized and refined as the individual performs responsive behavior. In
other words, we learn to do thru doing" (1973, p. 207).

Spencer cast reading behavior in the broadest possible context, as
Thorndike and Huey had suggested but had not articulated. It was not
that we should fail to be concerned with learning to read print, but that
we should see it in that broad context. "The educative process," he
wrote, "is primarily concerned with the development and refinement of
reading-behavior. That one will read is assured by nature. BUT, WHAT
one will read and HOW EFFECTIVELY the reading will be performed
are major concerns for the educative process" (1973, p. 207). Like Spencer, Huey, Thorndike, and others who have questioned defining reading
as a highly specialized mode of behavior, I am convinced that it is
instead a generic form of human behavior. That view assumes the reader is actively seeking to create meaning and to find order in reading.
Skill can be developed and enhanced or refined only in the service of this
drive.

A Different View

In the previous chapter, the conventional notion that learning to
read involves the acquisition of a series of arbitrary associations through
a process of decoding print to sound was contrasted with what was
termed an experiential or *naturalistic* view of the reading process. The
idea that language in all its forms can be evoked with little or no formal
instruction, given an appropriate environment, had its origins in the
progressive movement that swept American life following the Civil War.
The first comprehensive and systematic discussion of this view of reading appeared, as I have also noted in Chapter 1, in Edmund Burke
Huey's book, *The Psychology and Pedagogy of Reading*, first published
in 1908. Huey attacked conventional methods of instruction, charging
they were, like "an old curiosity shop of absurd practices" (p. 9), inefficient and wasteful of a child's time. Instead, he argued, children should
be taught at home, in an entirely informal manner. "The natural method of learning to read," he wrote, "is just the same as that of learning to
talk" (p. 330). To him, the child would pick up on reading simply by
having good, well-illustrated books read aloud in a responsive atmosphere.

And what if the child is denied the opportunity at home? In Huey's
mind, that was simple enough: The school should replicate the ideal
home environment. Even fewer homes provided that kind of situation
then than they do now. As well, only a handful of teachers were able to

translate those ideas into practice. Teaching by the textbook has always provided a much surer guide for the classroom teacher and the administrator. Today, when publishers have developed extensive support systems to which the teacher can turn at every step of a reading lesson, it is not surprising that pressure continues to follow the instructions contained in them.

Despite the politics engendered by what has become a sort of military-industrial complex in reading, in which the economic interests of authors/professors/teachers of instructional materials have become entwined with the publishing industry and the bureaucracy administering a vast school system, interest in naturalistic or experiential approaches to literacy has never completely disappeared. However, until the 1950s, advocacy of this different view of reading (and more recently of writing) relied mainly, as I have intimated, on an old propaganda technique known as The Testimonial.

Following World War II, Willard C. Olson (1959), a psychologist at the University of Michigan, proposed that children engage in "seeking, self-selection, and pacing" activities as a natural part of their development, and that this was equally true in the learning-to-read process. Additionally, he claimed that the course of reading development was unique to each child and that an appropriate reading curriculum would provide for these differences. Out of his ideas grew the first systematic rationale for a very different kind of instructional setting. Instead of being presented with a textbook that served as the basis for instruction in group settings, pupils would be free to select books of their own choice, reading them at a rate comfortable to each. The teacher would then give needed assistance primarily on an individual basis. Hence, the terms *seeking, self-selection*, and *pacing*. The *practice* instead of the *study* of reading became of central importance in the learning-to-read process, in large part replacing, but not excluding, formal instruction. And of course, the curriculum became individualized. Where conventional instruction relied primarily upon teaching children in groups presumed to be of similar ability or skill development, "self-selection," as it came to be known, called for individual and occasionally small-group instruction based on common interests or specific skill needs.

The notion of individualization became popular in the late 1950s, continuing on through the 1960s, although it found favor in hardly more than 4% or 5% of American elementary school classrooms. However, the scientific rationale Olson had provided led to a rash of studies designed to evaluate its effectiveness. Most of these were carried out by "converts," and due to the considerable problems inherent in conducting studies of teaching methods, which plague the schooling process generally, the results were seen as suspect by traditionalists. Still, we can say with some certainty that, in general, children taught in this way seemed to score on reading tests as well as or slightly better than children taught through textbooks. Since school people are rarely attracted to an alternative curriculum that can promise nothing more than parity on test scores — particularly where the intensity of the teaching process is multiplied, as is true of any "individualized" instructional program — it is not surprising that, despite its attractiveness to many teachers, "self-selection" failed to change teaching habits in a substantial way.

Obstacles to Change

But the beginnings of a scientific rationale for a naturalistic approach to the learning-to-read process had been established. As we shall see in subsequent chapters, new knowledge about the course of language development, and about the nature of children's thought, rationality, psychobiology, and physiology of growth and development, began to flood the educational scene. As I have also suggested, however, change is not easily achieved in schools. Departing from traditional practice often takes more energy than we are able to summon up. Inertia usually wins the day. It remains true, nonetheless, that many more teachers would like to embark on what might promise to be a more productive course where the teaching of reading is concerned. We might, at the least, confront one major obstacle to change. I have termed it the "military-industrial complex" in reading, a series of intertwined vested interests that dictate the American reading curriculum. Central among these is a large cadre of professionals, reading experts whose teaching and, to a certain extent, research are interlocked with preparing commercially successful instructional materials.

A second "vested interest" is the publishing industry itself. Powerful economic forces are at work in American society that continue to foster the influence of this industry in our schools. We have experienced a communications explosion over the past quarter of a century, and publishing houses now produce complex sets of integrated materials designed to completely engulf every aspect of what might be called the "reading curriculum." The day of a rather uncomplicated series of textbooks, workbooks, and teachers' manuals is gone; now we find comprehensive packages that, because of their complexity, require a further lengthening of the amount of time students spend in "studying" reading. Mergers and acquisitions have reduced competition and, as a result, the variety of instructional materials available to schools. A very few con-glomerates now publish a large majority of our books, but under a number of different "house" names to give each the illusion of an inde-pendent company (see Coser et al., 1982). "Reading" is big business in America.

The third "vested interest" is the school itself, which has increasing-ly relied upon prepared instructional materials in all areas. Teachers have to a very large extent become managers or directors of pre-pack-aged instructional materials. Then there are pressures emanating from within the school itself, from peers and from administrators who feel acutely the public's wrath over the apparent failure of schools generally to solve the problem of reading. Individual teachers, for example, feel strong pressures to conform, to teach as the others on the faculty do. There is a very real concern that the children be ready for the next teacher at the end of the year, and the best way to assure that is to teach in a fashion compatible with one's peers. Expectations govern behavior more often than we like to admit.

Administrators, most of whom are minimally knowledgeable about the reading curriculum, have learned to put their faith primarily in the instructional materials and only secondarily in the teaching competence of the faculty. After all, publishers give every assurance that their prod-uct is effective — "teacher-proof" as the saying goes. Even the least able teacher should succeed if the program of instruction prescribed by the teacher's manual and other support systems supplied by the publisher is followed. Not satisfied with this, many building principals and other school district officials frequently require additional evidence of what they believe — often incorrectly — marks progress in learning to read. For example, it is not uncommon, as I have already noted, to require that children be able to recognize in an isolated list — frequently one appear-ing in the textbook — the so-called "new words" contained in the text, a rote exercise that has the potential for depreciating the role of meaning in reading. Then, test scores are commonly used to measure individual teaching success.

It is little wonder, therefore, that traditional modes of instruction persist, often despite teachers' wishes to embark on a different path. Nor is it odd that the vast majority of the elementary school classrooms in the United States bear an uncanny similarity to one another. The materials we have given to teachers and the demands we place on them for con-formity leave little leeway. Perhaps the most notable difference within the vast structure of the American school system is to be found in the accents of the children, although mass media are rapidly reducing even these regional differences. Certainly, we find the same instructional materials somewhere in each of the 50 states, and we find teachers who have been taught how to teach in much the same fashion. Only now and then does the educational landscape show any noticeable variation.

However, disenchantment over the apparent continuing failure to generate sufficiently high levels of literacy is now leading to a much stronger interest than ever before in seeking an alternative to traditional practices. Previously, these alternatives were known by such terms as "self-selection," or "individualized" reading. In another form the alternative was referred to as "the language-experience approach" to the teaching of reading. In its present metamorphosis, the terminology has changed, to "whole language" and "literature-based" instruction. All find their basis in naturalistic or experiential concepts of the learning-to-read process. As policy develops among administrative units regarding how to respond to what is, so far, essentially political pressure toward solving an endemic educational problem, publishers are organizing to find ways of meeting changes in policy while also attempting to adjust to the demands of teachers who must implement that policy in the classroom. If history is to be our guide, we should expect that an attempt will be made to create a new form of the traditional reading textbook. Publishers and the other members of that "complex" which has very largely controlled reading instruction will find ways of organizing books and stories written primarily for the pleasure of children into the familiar textbook format. The textbooks of a "literature-based" reading program will revive the demand for multiple copies so necessary to profits in the textbook publishing industry. The textbook stories will then be taught page by page—all of the traditional practices will be reborn. And in fact a new addition to the "educationese" is beginning to appear to describe this process: the "basalization" of children's literature is underway, meaning that ways are already being found to incorporate literature written for children into the traditional textbook format.

Related Readings

Bettelheim, B., & Zela, K. (1982). *On learning to read: The child's fascination with meaning.* New York: Knopf.

Bettelheim, B. (1976). *The uses of enchantment.* New York: Vintage Books.

Chomsky, C. (1970). Reading, writing, and phonology. *Harvard Educational Review, 40,* 287–309.

Compaine, B. M. (1978). *The book industry in transition: An economic study of book distribution and marketing.* New York: Knowledge Industry Publications.

Crowhurst, M. (1979). Developing syntactic skills: Doing what comes naturally. *Language Arts, 56,* 522–525.

Davison, A., & Kantor, R. N. (1982). On the failure of readability formulas to define readable texts: A case study from adaptations. *Reading Research Quarterly, 17,* 187–211.

Dewey, J. (1900). *The school and society.* New York: University of Chicago Press.

Dewey, J. (1902). *The child and the curriculum.* Chicago: University of Chicago Press.

Dewey, J. (1938). *Experience and education.* New York: Macmillan.

Downing, J., & Leong, C. K. (1982). *Psychology of reading.* New York: Macmillan.

Downing, J. (1972). The cognitive clarity theory of learning to read. In V. Southgate (Ed.), *Literacy at all levels* (pp. 38–45). London: Ward Lock.

Eisner, E. W. (1976). Reading and the creation of meaning. In M. P. Douglass (Ed.), *Claremont Reading Conference, 40th Yearbook* (pp. 1–15). Claremont, CA: The Claremont Graduate School.

Fraatz, M. B. (1987). *The politics of reading: Power, opportunity and prospects for change in America's public schools.* New York: Teachers College Press.

Furth, H. G. (1966). *Thinking without language: Psychological implications of deafness.* New York: The Free Press.

Gibson, E. (1965). Word recognition. *Science, 148,* 1066–1072.

Goodman, K. S., & Goodman, Y. M. (1979). Learning to read is natural. In L. B. Resnick & P. A. Weaver (Eds.), *Theory and practice of early reading* (vol. 1, pp. 137–154). Hillsdale, NJ: Lawrence Erlbaum.

Goodman, Y. M. (1983). Language, cognitive development, and reading behavior. In M. P. Douglass (Ed.), *Claremont Reading Conference, 47th Yearbook* (pp. 10–16). Claremont, CA: The Claremont Graduate School.

Halliday, M. A. K. (1973). *Explorations in the functions of language.* London: Edward Arnold.

Holdaway, D. (1979). *The foundations of literacy.* Gosford, NSW: Ashton Scholastic.

Hoskisson, K. (1979). Learning to read naturally. *Language Arts, 56,* 489–496.

Johnson, J., & Tamburrini, J. (1972). *Informal reading and writing.* New York: Macmillan.

Kavanaugh, J. F., & Mattingly, I. G. (Eds.). (1972). *Language by eye and by ear.* Cambridge, MA: MIT Press.

Kerfoot, J. B. (1916). *How to read.* New York: Houghton Mifflin Company.

Shuy, R. (1981). Four misconceptions about clarity and simplicity. *Language Arts, 58,* 557–561.

Smith, F. (1982). *Understanding reading: A psycholinguistic analysis of reading and learning to read* (3rd ed.). New York: Holt, Rinehart & Winston.

Spencer, P. L. (1970). *Reading reading.* Claremont, CA: College Press.

Waller, T. G., & McKinnon, G. E. (Eds.). (1979). *Reading research: Advances in theory and practice.* New York: Academic Press.

Williams, J. P. (1973). Learning to read: A review of theories and models. *Reading Research Quarterly, 8,* 121–146.

CHAPTER 3

Two Incompatible Views

We are now seeing with much greater clarity how differently the problem of reading is being viewed. Although classroom practice has yet to feel the impact of the dichotomy that is becoming increasingly apparent among theorists in the field, it cannot be postponed indefinitely, much as the many vested interests in reading might wish it to be. While the division between these two very different views of reading, first outlined in the work of Huey and Spencer, was largely ignored for many years, the recent period (since the early 1960s) of intensive research makes it very unlikely such disregard can continue, if only because there are so many involved in elaborating upon these positions and because the dialogue in professional circles is becoming so heated.

We can characterize the basic issue that divides the world of reading in a number of different ways. However, it is all caught up in the question of whether function, as the conventional wisdom has always contended and as practice has traditionally observed, follows form, or, contrariwise, whether form follows function. Does one develop proficiency in reading printed words primarily as a consequence of learning the *skills* that logical deduction tells us can be associated with reading behavior? Or does skill in reading evolve differently, emerging (as the naturalistic view contends) primarily from the need or desire to read? Evidence is increasingly being offered in support of *both* positions, which suggests that basic philosophical presuppositions underlie the point of view one is attracted to. That is, while we may refer to research, and even conduct some ourselves, we begin in the field of reading, just as we do in every other endeavor, with certain assumptions that become dislodged only in the face of evidence so incontrovertible as to shake the most basic of beliefs. Such research can of course serve another purpose, and that is to give substance to only partially formed ideas, to confirm "sneaking suspicions" as it were.

Reductionism versus Constructivism

In explaining the fundamental conceptual differences that separate traditional views from the naturalistic or experiential approach to language learning, the Kantian notion of *constructivism*, that "we come to know our world by actively constructing it rather than by passively taking it in," is increasingly being used as a theoretical point of departure for thinking about the problem of reading (Shuy, 1981, p. 102). In contrast, the traditional view—in the Kantian terminology again, *reductionism*—assumes "that behavior must be reduced to its most elementary parts before these parts can be combined to understand more complex behavior" (p. 102). The constructivist view also asserts the importance of social context in learning, while the reductionist tends to see behavior more or less isolated from context. To illustrate, phonics advocates, at least in the initial stages of teaching and learning, disregard the importance of context; whole-word approaches, since they purport to present words because they are more meaningful units, can be said to consider context in a limited sense, but only that, because motivation to read and the social setting in which it occurs are based primarily on extrinsic rather than intrinsic elements. Thus we see the traditional or reductionist view assuming reading behavior to be acquired primarily through the learning of the parts of reading that logical analysis has identified as composing the total, complex behavior, divorced, entirely or in major part, from the context in which reading itself is to occur. Traditional teaching practices, while concerned about motivating children to read, are more interested in motivation as it relates to tackling a particular instructional lesson than to the larger context, that is, reading qua reading. The naturalistic or experiential approach—also currently being called an "holistic" approach to reading—assumes the reader is actively seeking to create meaning and find order in reading. Skill is developed and enhanced or refined in the service of this drive. The emphasis upon intrinsic forms of motivation and reward or satisfaction stands in sharp contrast to the reductionist reliance upon extrinsic motivation and rewards.

To reiterate in yet another way, the holistic or constructivist view is one in which the whole is equal to *more* than the sum of its parts. The reductionist position, in contrast, sees the whole to be neither more nor less than the sum of its parts.

What these "world views" may mean as far as learning to read words in their printed form will become clearer as we look at examples of some models developed to illustrate different theoretical notions about what is happening when "reading" is said to be taking place. As we do this, it may still be necessary to remind ourselves that these models are indeed only *theoretical* representations of reading behavior. We *do not* know exactly what occurs when reading takes place, and so any attempt to describe this behavior must necessarily consist of educated guesses. Still, the development of models such as these marks an important stage in the evolution of our understanding of reading behavior. In addition to suggesting the diversity of views currently held in this regard, they also illuminate the polarization of thinking in the field. The most important contribution of such "model-making" has been the provision of points of departure for research that will ultimately shed important light on the problem of reading itself. But it should be remembered that, whatever forthcoming research seems to say to us, all such research begins with a premise or assumption about the nature of reading behavior that reflects the division, even chasm, between reductionist and constructivist conceptions. In other words, the evidence research makes available to us may well be based on objective or empirical data, but the premise behind it necessarily remains subjective and value-laden.

The Reductionist View of Reality

Within the reductionist position we will first look to the work of Jack Holmes, which has been further developed and refined by his student, Harry Singer. Holmes began the development of what he eventually was to call "The Substrata-Factor Theory of Reading" as a doctoral student in the late 1940s at the University of California at Berkeley, where he was subsequently to teach until his untimely death in 1965. Holmes first sought to isolate factors basic to the ability to read print. He began this process by reviewing over 500 experimental studies for a list of factors that might be considered causal in success or failure in learning to read. From this review he identified 80 such variables, to which he then proceeded to apply several complex statistical procedures to identify the most significant for reading. Between 1948 and 1965, Holmes and his students fleshed out the substrata-factor theory model of reading through progressive refinement of statistical processes, ending up with a highly detailed schema depicting what they believed to be the essential elements in reading behavior. Ultimately, they were able to assign values suggesting the relative importance of each of these factors at various stages of reading development. Figure 3.1 presents only one part of the model — the total model is too complicated to present in this context, setting forth as it does a highly complex set of interrelationships that vary throughout the span of grade levels.

The inference one is likely to gain from this model is that it is but a very short step to the classroom; it is clear that teaching should develop the strengths of each of the factors and work on the weaknesses the model helps identify, stressing each in relation to its presumed relative

FIGURE 3.1.   The Substrata-Factor Theory Model of Reading

Diagrammatic model of the substrata-factors accompanying development of power of reading in
grades 3 to 6. The model shows for each grade the first level substrata factors and their percent
contributions to variance in power of reading. The variance *not* accounted for is probably attributable
to attitudinal factors, verbal flexibility, and mobilizers.

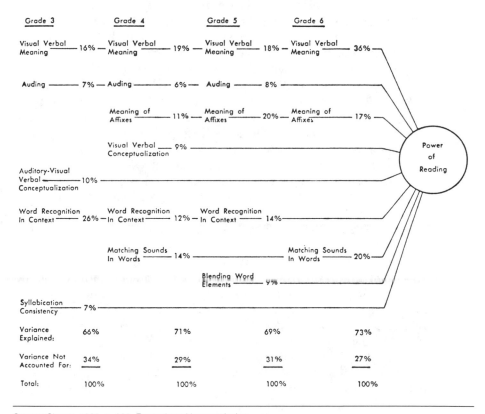

Source: Singer, 1985, p. 625. Reproduced by permission.

importance. The primary emphasis is consequently upon the development of isolable skill elements; the initial focus is on the parts of words,
and the ultimate "basic unit" of reading is the individual word. Thus
neither the context in which individual words are imbedded — as they
are in sentences, paragraphs — nor the meaning of the reading matter
itself plays a direct part in this particular theory of reading. Mastery of
the reading act is instead perceived as gaining control over the various
parts in roughly the degree to which each is seen as participating in

reading behavior at any particular stage of reading development. The problem of reading, therefore, becomes one of achieving a successful synthesis of all the different "factors" in reading behavior.

Our second example of a reductionist conception of reading is a more recent one proposed by LaBerge and Samuels (1985). It falls under the rubric of an "information-processing" model in that it attempts to identify the salient characteristics or features of print and how children use these to recognize words. The researchers assume that, at the beginning stages, the children must give conscious attention to each detail as they learn to associate symbol (x) with its sound (x^1). Gradually this rather rudimentary ability to achieve sound-symbol correspondence gives way to the automatic processing of visual "information" — that is, the child learns the $x=x^1$ equation in its various printed representations, primarily through the psychological process of association, or the stimulus-response (S-R) bond described briefly in Chapter 1. The purpose in learning to read is simply to reach the point at which this equation is learned well enough that the result is the automatic processing of the visual stimuli, the "information" appearing on the page. Thus the goal of reading is the development of "automaticity," the processing of visual information so automatically the reader no longer needs to give attention to the mechanics of reading — which has consumed the beginning stages — but can now direct attention toward meaning. Learning to read, then, means learning to move *toward* comprehension, but the learning-to-read process itself does not begin with meaning. Instead, it starts with the details of learning how to process those elements of visual information that LaBerge and Samuels consider to be the most significant. For them, this means mastering visual information ranging from knowledge of the height and width of individual letters (on the assumption this is essential in discriminating such letters as m from n, and b from d, and so on) to gaining information about overall word configuration and knowledge of spelling patterns.

The various figures developed by LaBerge and Samuels to illustrate their "model" are complex and employ terminology that only a few researchers familiar with their studies can use freely and intelligently. Within the basic model, details can be changed to represent the different kinds of information processing conditions they have identified. At the risk of oversimplifying and in the process distorting the model, we can see the basic elements fairly clearly in Figure 3.2.

The LaBerge-Samuels view, increasingly shared by other reductionists, is that reading involves much more than a simple sound-letter correspondence response, that one must consider sound-spelling units *within* words, along with the visual configuration itself — not simply the

FIGURE 3.2.   The LaBerge and Samuels "Information-Processing" Model of Reading

Representation of associative links between codes in visual memory (VM), phonological memory (PM), episodic memory (EM), and the response system (RS). Attention is momentarily focused on a code in visual memory.

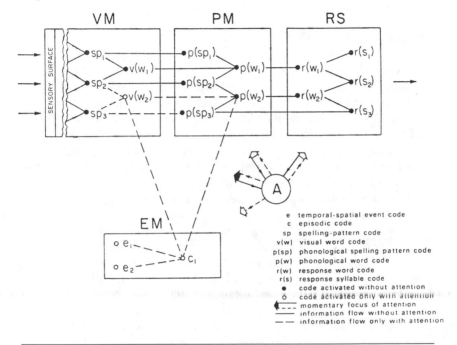

e   temporal-spatial event code
c   episodic code
sp   spelling-pattern code
v(w)   visual word code
p(sp)   phonological spelling pattern code
p(w)   phonological word code
r(w)   response word code
r(s)   response syllable code
•   code activated without attention
ò   code activated only with attention
◄--- momentary focus of attention
——   information flow without attention
— —   information flow only with attention

Source: LaBerge & Samuels, 1985, p. 701. Reproduced by permission.

overall shape, but the formation of individual letters that are presumed to provide significant clues to the process of decoding. This term, *decoding*, has come to be used as a descriptor of the overall process of converting words in their printed form into their auditory representations. However, as the LaBerge-Samuels models suggests, the identification of numerous elements within this process has led to a recognition that it is complex and cannot be viewed as a simple question of developing appropriate sound-symbol correspondences. This in turn has led to the development of a new "scientific" base for justifying "synthetic" methods of instruction, adding to the justification of that approach inherited from old-style phonics advocates from days long past.

In summary, then, the reductionist view holds that learning to read is accomplishcd primarily through a process of synthesis, and that this process is essentially a passive one. The problem for the learner is to acquire knowledge and skill preselected from an analysis of the desired behavior; the learning process itself then involves the achievement of a synthesis into a whole.

The Constructivist View of Reality

Although the constructivist view of reality is usually attributed to eighteenth-century philosopher Immanuel Kant (1724–1804), with credit for its more modern interpretation given to twentieth-century thinker Ludwig Wittgenstein (1889–1951), its origins can be traced to Aristotle, and perhaps before. To the constructivist, learning consists of acquiring knowledge and skills largely through personal experiencing, and not as a consequence of association in response to external stimuli largely out of the control of the learner. In language learning — in all its forms, including the learning of a second language — this means one gains knowledge and skill primarily through reading, speaking, writing, and listening themselves. One quite literally learns to read by reading; one "constructs" knowledge and skill about the process almost exclusively, if not entirely, through one's own individual efforts. Thus, one's purpose, one's desire to create meaning, and the context in which language behavior is learned are all critical (Magoon, 1977).

As I have previously suggested, the attempt to develop models of the reading process has been critical in directing research and in sharpening our perceptions of differences in our understandings of the nature of reading behavior. Interestingly, Spencer, who viewed the reading of printed words as essentially the same as all other forms of knowing, was the first to develop a model of reading, which he did in the 1930s. He published a simplified version a number of years later, asserting the reading process could be "structurally pictured" as the series of steps shown in Figure 3.3 (Spencer, 1961).

In Spencer's model we see what is common to all constructivist views, namely, the emphasis placed on meaning; only incidentally does the nature of the stimulus appear in it. We should also take note, although it is not self-evident in the model, that Spencer emphasized the dynamic nature of reading, what he termed a "continuous behavior process," which, once begun, sets up a dynamic tension that then feeds upon itself, demanding that it continue.

Perhaps the most widely known constructivist currently is Kenneth S. Goodman. Goodman describes himself as a "psycholinguist," one who seeks to meld information from two previously disparate fields of

FIGURE 3.3. Spencer's Model of Reading

STIMULUS	STIMULATION	PERCEPTION	EXPRESSION
Any thing which activates any sense receptor.	The activation of sense receptors. Transforming non-neural impulses into neural impulses.	Cognition, recognition, association, creating meaning, giving significance, formulating plan of action, activating and directing response mechanisms.	Performing the adaptive responses as directed; e.g., orally expressing the words and word patterns as perceived under visual stimulation.

Source: Spencer, 1960, p. 5.

inquiry, psychology and linguistics, using that blend of information to achieve a new understanding of the nature of reading behavior. Like most constructivists interested in the problem of reading, Goodman is attracted to and uses a metaphor for understanding the relationship between language and its representational forms that was developed by Noam Chomsky, one of the most distinguished if controversial of modern linguistic scholars. With its notions of *deep structure* and *surface structure*, Chomsky's work has revolutionized the field of linguistics and made available powerful new tools for theorizing about how language is generated and, consequently, learned. In the Chomsky lexicon, surface structure refers to the obvious features of a language—the sounds utilized in spoken language, for example, or the grammatical rules that a language appears to follow. Deep structure, in contrast, refers to the meaning implicit in the surface structure, the rules that are hidden from view, the subtleties of the language (Chomsky, 1970). Consider the following two examples: In the first set, the surface structure of the statement is different, yet the meaning remains the same; in the second set, the surface structure remains the same, but the meaning changes as a function of a one-word change:

Example 1   (a) John went with his father to play golf.
             (b) John's dad went to the links with him.
Example 2   (a) John is easy to please.
             (b) John is easy to see.

Goodman thinks reading print is akin to listening. One learns by selecting and anticipating in a rule-governed setting. That is, language is governed by a set of rules that the reader anticipates and uses as a guide in generating meanings. In other words, we know what constitutes a sentence or intelligible phrase, and what is not an intelligible statement. Certain words cannot follow certain other words, and vice versa. Selecting from what one knows about language, one evolves a tacit understanding of the rules governing oral language and then applies these rules in print-reading (or writing) situations. Employing those rules, along with other cues drawn from our capacity to use oral language, the reader anticipates meanings and in the process constructs new meanings as the reading proceeds. In this view, not only can true reading not take place without meaning, but it is the meaning generated by reading that makes the further development of reading skill possible.

Goodman (1976b) has described reading as "a psycholinguistic guessing game," an unfortunate use of the word *guessing*, in my estimation, since it suggests a more random activity than is really the case, as Goodman himself points out. The American penchant for catch-words has not bypassed educationists, and so the term has become a popular if misleading one in understanding Goodman's point of view.

Goodman and his wife and colleague, Yetta Goodman, have sought to understand reading behavior by studying miscues in oral reading; that is, they have examined the nature of children's "errors" in oral reading to discover their characteristics and, hence, to conjecture upon their sources (Goodman, 1969). Fluent readers, for example, frequently substitute a word of similar meaning for one appearing in the text, in the process making the "error" of changing the surface structure, but not altering the meaning. Since the constructivist view's primary concern is meaning, errors of this order cannot be considered true mistakes. The Goodmans have sought to understand those mistakes that might be thought of as true errors, namely, where a word that does not fit the context of the sentence is substituted for the "correct" one. From such analyses Goodman (1976a) has hypothesized the model for reading shown in Figure 3.4.

Goodman's model is a complex one and, like others, is a theoretical construct only, a "tentative" model at best. When one compares it with the other models discussed here, particularly reductionist models, one is struck by the importance Goodman gives to meaning, context, and affect, and the relative lack of significance these are given in the others. Here we see extensive attention given to the deep structure, and relatively little to the configurational aspects of language and to the mechanics of the reading process.

Another person widely associated with a constructivist view of reading is Frank Smith, a professor at the University of Victoria in British Columbia. Smith and Goodman both conceive of reading as a "psycholinguistic guessing game," anticipatory within a rule-governed frame. Both emphasize that, since language is rule-governed, reading

FIGURE 3.4. The Goodman Model of Reading

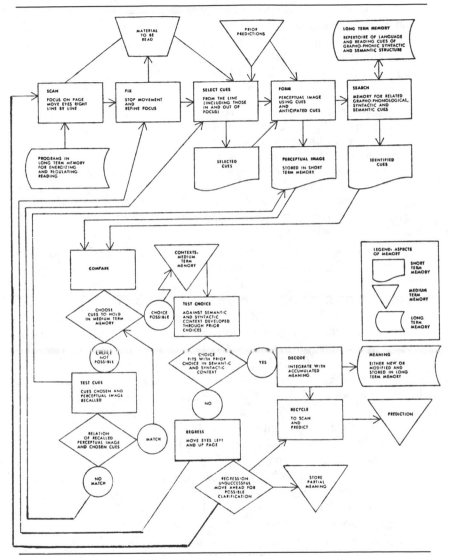

Source: Goodman, 1976a, p. 491. Reproduced by permission.

becomes the process by which one makes tentative hypotheses, utilizing only the minimum number of clues possible, anticipating ("guessing") what each succeeding word in a meaningful phrase may be. Unlike Goodman, Smith has not attempted to devise a model of reading in the sense I have been using the term here, saying, in effect, the process is too complex to do justice to it in that form. According to Smith (1982)

> there is nothing special about reading in terms of what a reader has to do. Reading does not make any exclusive or esoteric demands on the brain. There are no unique kinds of movements that the eyes must make in reading that they do not make when we examine a picture or glance around a room. . . . And there is nothing exceptional about the language that we read either, . . . nothing the brain must do to make sense of language that is written that it does not do to comprehend speech. There is not even anything distinctive about learning how to read. (p. 1)

Smith believes that trying to commit information *about* reading to memory is counterproductive to the learning-to-read process; doing so leaves children more confused than when they began. Reading is an activity of reconstructing experience: The reader brings meaning *to* the printed page. As Spencer argued long ago, one does not get meaning from reading; rather, meanings are quite literally created within the mind of the reader during this activity, and they are only as rich and varied — and meaningful — as the reader can make them. The art of writing, therefore, is the art of selecting and arranging words with the greatest potential of evoking richness and variety in the reader's mind.

Smith (1982) is particularly articulate regarding the role of sound (or more properly its lack of a role) in reading; to Smith, the process is not one of decoding to sound, as the LaBerge-Samuels model would have it, but reading aloud is really only redundant confirmation that reading itself has *already* taken place. In this view, "an analysis of the relationships between print and speech shows that the 'rules' relating spelling to the sounds of speech in English are . . . largely irrelevant to reading in any language" (p. 2). Smith goes on to argue:

> Reading is less a matter of extracting sound from print than of bringing meaning to print. The sounds that are supposed to reveal the meaning of sequences of letters cannot . . . be produced unless a probable meaning can be determined in advance. It is a universal fact of reading rather than a defect of English spelling that the effort to read through decoding is largely futile and unnecessary. (p. 2)

According to Smith, it is not phonics that makes reading possible; rather, it is reading that makes phonics appear to work. He points out that the pronunciation of words often depends upon the context in which they appear (*lead, read, sow, wound*), and this fact defies the simple logic of phonics, as do other seeming anomalies—for example, the *oo* "sound" in *cook, broom, blood,* and *stood*; the *ph* sound in *telephone* and *haphazard*; the *sh* in *bishop* and *mishap*. All these, not to mention the dialect differences that mark Bostonese off from the Southern "drawl" and the Midwestern "twang," prove Smith's case.

Smith (1978) sums up his view of reading by claiming, "we learn to read by reading, conducting experiments as we go along" (p. 97). In other words, children gain proficiency as they test hypotheses about language and how it is rendered in its printed form on the basis of the context or the meaning they can generate *as they read*. They develop a number of strategies to do this. They predict what a word may mean from context or analogy, or they skip it, postponing the problem of meaning with regard to a particular word. Through this sort of process the youngsters are, quite literally, teaching themselves to read, much as they learned to talk and to listen. The teacher/coach's role, then, is to help when help is sought by the learner, to foster and encourage, but *not* get in the youngster's way.

Conflict in the Reading Place

While conflict is in the nature of the human condition, too much of it is disconcerting when planning a course of action. In fact, much of human effort seems directed toward reducing the conflicting elements in our lives. We may therefore be dismayed to discover that the problem of reading introduces yet another set of conflicts into our lives: fundamentally different perceptions regarding the nature of the problem of reading and, as a consequence, how it should be resolved in the classroom. It is a healthy sign, nonetheless, that the nature of the perceptions that divide professional opinion are at last becoming clarified. Once those differences are out in the open, it becomes possible to respond in a more rational fashion.

Conflict arising from the divergent views of the learning-to-read process comes to a head when we attempt to select a response to the situation: Should teaching be structured to *invoke* or to *evoke* this behavior? After all, the problem of reading has been with us for a very long time. Surely, these issues should have been known and worked out long ago. Perhaps we need to recall the fact that we have only recently had the tools to study reading behavior in any depth. For the better part of the almost 100 years in which reading has been a professional concern, those involved in the problem have been either educationists or psychologists, many of whom were at the same time wearing two or more hats. I referred earlier to a "military-industrial complex" in reading, and it is appropriate here to remind ourselves that it has not been uncommon for college teachers of reading to find themselves with deep economic interests in a particular set of instructional materials, which they have written in their role as "reading specialists," while also teaching current and future teachers regarding the best ways to instruct children. Such obvious conflicts of interest were, and remain, common; at the same time they have gone relatively unnoticed as a potential barrier to furthering understanding of the reading process. Happily, the study of reading has in the recent past become an enterprise of interest to many people from diverse backgrounds. The result has been more objective inquiry into the nature of the problem.

Still, there are fundamental differences in the way the problem of reading can be addressed. I have categorized these differences under two distinctive views of reality, the reductionist and the constructivist. As discussed in Chapter 2, philosophic commitments and vested interests, particularly where the reductionist position resides, combine with traditional practices such that there remains a great deal of pressure to maintain the status quo. Thus the common response to the reading problem today is to refine and intensify practices that have long been part of the classroom scene.

My own constructivist orientation leads me, as I have written, to view reading as a generic form of behavior, one of creating meanings through the various sense modalities with which human beings have been endowed. Some have been denied optimum use of those avenues to knowing the world, some severely so, yet I believe sensitivity to the role of the sense modalities, individually and collectively, will suggest ways for all to become effective and fluent readers. Creating meanings, the process of reading, is totally dependent upon experience and experiencing. That is where all the meanings, the "knowings" we have, come from. And that is what we bring to new situations, to our experiencing of today, as we build our understanding of the world and where we fit into it. Consequently the *quality* of our experiencing has everything to do with the depth and richness with which we understand. New meanings become available to us, then, as we have the opportunity to rub our prior experiences, available to us as thoughts, together; it is not unlike rubbing two sticks together to get fire.

Unfortunately, the word *experience*, in its educational context, at least, has for many a negative connotation. Much of that is due to the contentious arguments that have taken place over the years as professional and lay persons tried to assimilate or dispose permanently of one of John Dewey's most provocative ideas (see, for example, Dewey, 1938). Dewey complicated life for us by pointing out the importance of experience in learning, not only what has actively "happened" to us, but also what we have felt and thought as individuals. Experience is not given to us by someone else, and one cannot share an experience completely, because it is personal; what any experience means to us depends upon what has happened earlier on, what we are like now, and how the two conditions interact. Experiences consequently shape each person in unique ways no matter how similar they may seem to those others have had.

When attempts were made to translate Dewey's insights into classroom practice, this broad view of the nature and significance of "experience" was often too narrowly conceived. Experience was thought to exist entirely in overt activity, and the concept became equated with noise and disorder in the classroom. The broader meaning and significance of the concept became lost in the outcries of enraged adults who conceived of learning as a passive, orderly affair best conducted in silence. Learning was not thought of as the reconstruction of experience, as Dewey would have had it. Instead, the learner was thought of as a near empty vessel into which knowledge would be poured. The acquisition of knowledge, not learning as such, provided the primary focus for classroom activity. Although "experience" was given lip service, the true focus was on preparation for the future, on getting ready for the next grade, on preparing for "life," as if school were not life, but a place where one prepared for the real thing.

Reading words in their printed form is one kind of experience, one way of thinking, if one adopts the Deweyan view. Writing provides another "kind" of thinking (or experience), one that is not fundamentally different from reading, despite a few obvious (although inconsequential) differences. Speaking and listening can be thought of in the same fashion. These kinds of experience draw upon a uniquely human endowment: the ability to refer to experience through the use of language and to use that experience in thought, reorganizing and restructuring it for whatever purposes may drive the reader/language user at the time. There are of course a multitude of other kinds of experience; we find them in the arts, in nature, in human relationships, in every aspect of life. Thus personal experiencing becomes a commodity that is not useful to anyone else, except in an indirect fashion. As teachers, it may guide us in enhancing the quality of others' experience. To speak of reading as the reconstruction of experience, then, it is to say that reading is learning (or reasoning, as Thorndike pointed out so long ago).

Related Readings

Allen, J. P. B., & VanBuren, P. (Eds.). (1971). *Chomsky: Selected readings.* Cambridge: Oxford University Press.

DiSibio, M. (1982). Memory for connected discourse: A constructivist view. *Review of Educational Research, 52,* 149–174.

Fraatz, M. G. (1987). *The politics of reading: Power, opportunity and prospects for change in America's public schools.* New York: Teachers College Press.

Goodman, K. S., & Flemming, J. T. (Eds.). (1969). *Psycholinguistics and the teaching of reading.* Newark, DE: International Reading Association.

Goodman, K. S., & Goodman, Y. M. (1979). Learning about psycholinguistic processes by analyzing oral reading. *Harvard Educational Review, 47,* 317–333.

Goodman, K. S., & Goodman, Y. M. (1979). Learning to read is natural. In L. B. Resnick & P. A. Weaver (Eds.), *Theory and practice of early reading* (Vol. 1, pp. 137–154). Hillsdale, NJ: Lawrence Erlbaum.

Halliday, M. A. K. (1975). *Learning how to mean.* London: Edward Arnold.

Krashen, S. D. (1985). *The input hypothesis: Issues and implications.* New York: Longman.

Steinberg, D. D., & Yamada, J. (1978–1979). Are whole word kanji easier to learn than syllable kana? *Reading Research Quarterly, 14,* 88–99.

Vygotsky, L. S. (1962). *Mind in society* (M. Cole, V. John-Steiner, S. Scribner, & E. Souberman, Trans.). Cambridge, MA: Harvard University Press.

Williams, J. P. (1973). Learning to read: A review of theories and models. *Reading Research Quarterly, 8,* 121–146.

Yadon, D., & Templeton, S. (Eds.). (1986). *Metalinguistic awareness and beginning literacy: Conceptualizing what it means to read and write.* Portsmouth, NH: Heinemann Educational Books.

CHAPTER 4

The Three Faces of Reading

If there is anything we can be certain about where reading is concerned, it is the extraordinary complexity of this form of behavior and its uniqueness as a singularly human accomplishment. In sorting out the complexities of reading, we can think of it as having three major facets, or faces. These are (1) *the thing to be read*, (2) *the sensory modalities* that transform the stimulus into neural impulses, and (3) *the neuro-motor-cortical matrix* that makes thought possible and serves to direct the responses that all reading entails. In the following discussion, we will consider each of these in turn.

The Things We Read

Of the three facets, or faces, of reading, one lies completely outside of the learner, namely, the thing we seek to read. In previous chapters I have suggested that there appears to be an inherent human proclivity to make sense out of the world around us, and as humans over the ages have done this, various categories of signs and symbols have been invented to represent our understanding of the world. Human activity requires the presence of a shorthand to represent that reality, since it is only with this kind of symbolling and signing that we can perceive interrelationships within naturally occurring events and conditions. Those signs and symbols, but particularly the symbols, serve to represent knowledge derived from our experience in a number of ways. They serve most importantly as a means for communication and human interaction. They serve as well as a storehouse of human experiencing, so that each succeeding generation does not begin from scratch. While knowledge itself remains the private possession of individuals—it is not held collectively—symbols make it possible for us to reach a common level of experience and therefore understanding.

What I have said so far does not bind our thinking to any particular set of symbols. While it is true that the symbol system used to represent

one's first or primary language plays a distinctive role in relation to all
the others, I have already suggested that one would be hard-pressed to
identify anything unique about it. Although not all language groups
have created or invented a visual representation of their oral language,
the reason for the existence of such representations remains the same as
that for any "language": to create a way in which human experience can
be shared and recalled. Alex Haley's book, *Roots* (1976), popularized an
appreciation for the role of oral history at a time when languages more
often than not had no written representational system or, as was the case
in Europe at about the same time, when only the smallest fraction of the
population was literate. Among the famous illiterates of the thirteenth
century was none other than Charlemagne himself. And of course we
should not forget the story of Sequoia, who invented a written form of
his people's language where none had existed before, one which has
survived to this day.

Basic as the primary language is to human interaction, therefore, it
is still true that other representational systems abound, among them the
many different symbol systems we associate with mathematics, the natural sciences, musical notation, and dance. Because of the signal importance of the primary language in all human interaction, it is not surprising that we want to lend it special significance and, in turn, give a
unique role to the written or printed form of that language. Never mind
that there are almost countless numbers of different languages, and that
even though not all have written forms, an unusually wide array of
systems exist for representing them on a flat surface. Never mind as well
that we are much more inclined to think that one learns other symbol
systems by starting with the ideas that the symbol represents, rather
than with the particular form of the symbol, as is the case in teaching
children to read print. No amount of argument seems able to sway us
from the notion that there are qualities in the way the English language
is rendered on the page that make it the special case it is generally
considered to be. So perhaps we need once again to remind ourselves
that there is nothing really sacred about the way an oral/aural language
is written down.

Sense Modalities in Reading:
An Integrative Process

Reading is popularly considered to be a visual/auditory process,
and of these, the visual sense is considered the premier ability of the
two. The importance of hearing is seen not so much in the reading act

itself, but as the source for language: The ability to speak and to listen meaningfully depends upon an intact auditory system that is subsequently called into service as the reader seeks to "decode" symbol into sound. Print reading itself, then, is seen as stimulating an already existing sound system through visual pathways.

The traditional view has considered print reading to be almost entirely controlled by visual processes. That notion has also been enjoying increasing popularity among reading researchers in recent years. Part of this popularity is no doubt due to the availability of the eye for research purposes; one can control the variables, a most important criterion for scientific research. The "target" is more or less fixed and the response can be measured with relative ease. Hearing has been another matter, however, since that process is totally internalized. What is heard literally disappears into the brain, leaving little objective means of evaluating its effect.

Because researchers, as well as the public, have been attracted to the notion that reading is an act almost entirely controlled by the visual process, there has been a pronounced tendency to think of reading as a primarily mechanical, rather than creative or thinking, activity, at least during the initial stages in the learning-to-read process. In the La Berge/Samuels model of reading behavior discussed briefly in the previous chapter, for example, the great importance of what they term "visual information" is clearly implied, and we thus see concern over discovering all of the possible details of that "information," including the configurations of individual letters, because all are viewed as contributing in some kind of direct fashion. Presumably, such information is critical to the learning-to-read process and should therefore be considered in planning instruction.

The general public, and not a few teachers, have always held to the importance of seeing and reading. One still hears as a first recommendation where a reading problem is suspected the admonition to "see an eye doctor." Actually, visual problems are rarely the cause of reading problems. "Correcting" a problem, such as a poor near-point acuity (sharpness of seeing) may make reading a somewhat more comfortable activity, but it cannot be implicated as a cause of reading disability. If visual processing were the primary activity in reading print, we might reasonably expect persons with seriously impaired visual capacities to suffer from reading problems. Following the logic of this argument, one might then expect a person who is completely blind to be unable to read at all.

Yet blind people do "read," using Braille as a substitute for print. And so, just as mild visual disturbances rarely if ever prove to be the source of a reading problem, more severe impairments equally cannot be implicated. The reality of it is that persons with visual impairments so serious they are unable to process written symbols have no unusual problems in learning to read symbols representing human language, provided those symbols are compatible with the sensory avenues that remain available. In such instances, readers supplant the visual with the tactile and kinaesthetic. Interestingly, there are no reports of great difficulty being encountered in this kind of a learning-to-read situation. Since visually impaired people usually have intact hearing capabilities, they have no difficulty with oral language development, and this fact provides us with a clue regarding what is primary in the learning-to-read process.

Consider particularly the situation of people who have been profoundly deaf or even severely hard of hearing from the first year or two of life: They are denied the opportunity (which is available to both unimpaired and blind children) to store auditory images. The most obvious consequence of such a disability to the lay person is the difficulty most such individuals experience in articulating the sound system of the language they are attempting to speak. More significantly, such persons need to develop a substitute for the sound system possessed by individuals with intact sensory systems. Various methods of signing have developed over the years in attempts to find solutions to this problem, no one of which has gained universal approval. Recall that Helen Keller utilized a system of tactile-kinaesthetic signs to "spell out" her thoughts in Polly Thompson's hand. There is reason to believe that this was her primary means for rendering the language, although she did learn to speak; unfortunately, her speech was not at all clear, a fact she greatly regretted because she felt her lack of articulation reduced her ablility to communicate with others. However, she not only learned to speak in English, but in eight other languages as well. In any event, "finger spelling," which is read visually and in some instances tactilely, is gaining attention as a substitute for more traditional methods. Although perhaps not a complete substitute for storing images that stand for or represent one's primary language, it would appear that the visual and tactile-kinaesthetic sensory modes can successfully serve as nearly complete substitutes for the auditory images normally hearing people rely on in developing language power.

We see here additional evidence of the potency in the notion that the sense receptors are interacting with each other where language activity, of whatever kind, is taking place. In the classroom, we have known about this phenomenon for many years. In the 1930s, for example, Grace Fernald (1943) developed what she called a "tactile-kinaesthetic method" to help children with reading problems. In it, children were asked to write the word they wanted to "learn," perhaps in the air, but usually with the finger in contact with a textured surface, such as a sand table or a paper towel. The method has survived over the years because, in the experience of the teachers who have become aware of it, many children have been helped.

We can see, then, there are strong indicators that all of the sense receptors are involved to one degree or another in the reading process. We know, too, that the development of the sensitivity of these receptors is nearly unlimited. Persons denied the use of a particular receptor system invariably will increase their power to utilize remaining ones. The blind, for example, generally develop their tactile-kinaesthetic sensory systems far more than do those with intact sensory systems, and so on. In understanding reading behavior, we should be sensitive to the potential relative importance of each of the several sensory systems we have available to us. It is my contention that we have greatly overemphasized the role of visual processes in the reading of print. In fact, recent research demonstrates that the visual system is less sensitive than either the auditory or the tactile-kinaesthetic sensory modalities; it is neither capable of as wide a range of responses nor as quick to respond to stimulation, discrepancies being revealed through evoked potential and electrodiagnostic research (Davis, 1984; Robinson & Rudge, 1982). How significant those physiological differences are remains to be seen. But it hardly seems possible to avoid the conclusion that all of the sense receptors are acting in some kind of unison in all behavior. Learning, thinking, and therefore teaching, requires we consider that reality.

Vision and the Visual Process

While we cannot implicate visual anomalies as directly causal where problems in print reading are concerned, there are still good reasons to be aware of their potential for reducing personal/social and cognitive functioning. Visual acuity, the sharpness with which we see, can be impaired at either the near or the far point. Blurred vision when focusing on near objects is called *hyperopia*; the opposite condition — blurred vision when focusing on far objects — is called *myopia*. Both are fairly common occurrences in children. Hyperopia, in a reduction of acuity at the near point, may cause difficulties in reading print, but myopia, which affects distance vision, does not suggest a deleterious effect where print reading is concerned; however, restriction on seeing at a distance can limit the ability to see writing on a chalkboard and may thus cause other kinds of classroom work to suffer. It has sometimes been asserted that young children tend to be hyperopic (i.e., far-sighted) and that this condition has an effect on the early stages of learning to read. There is a modicum of truth in that observation, but it is so slight that we can dismiss the possibility of its having any significant influence.

Another visual anomaly sometimes found in children involves impairment in how well the two eyes function together; in technical terms this condition is called a *strabismus*. In years gone by, it was not uncommon to see an individual who was either "cross-eyed" (*endophoric*) or "wall-eyed" (*exophoric*). These problems are generally now successfully treated at a very early age with corrective lenses or through surgery, and so there are only a minuscule number of such cases among school-age children.

Yet another problem, rare but sufficiently present and important to warrant careful awareness, is a condition known as *amblyopia*. In this instance, the brain gradually reduces its capacity to receive the neural stimuli generated in the visual process. Why this occurs we are uncertain. The problem almost always presents itself in one eye, and so, without detection, can progress to the point where usable sight in the affected eye is lost permanently. Amblyopias most often begin to develop in youngsters around the age of 7 or 8, and so it is particularly important to be cognizant of the potential for this problem arising. To reverse the condition before permanent damage occurs, the eye doctor patches the "good eye," making the affected one "work harder." In most instances normal or near-normal sight is restored. While having sight in only one eye will not necessarily produce a reading problem, there are many other serious consequences that early detection can avoid, most notably a diminished ability to detect depth, which will interfere with any sports activity and may also affect driving.

Although these more commonly observed visual anomalies have not been identified as causal where reading problems are concerned, that does not mean no such relationships exist. They are, however, extraordinarily rare. One such instance is a condition known as *aniseikonia*, in which the ocular images are unequal either in size or shape in the two eyes. Alert parents will generally develop a concern for their child's visual health long before school entry, although teachers should also be aware of the possibilities in this regard. In my own experience as a teacher, for example, I once discovered a child in my fourth-grade class whose academic records listed him as having 20/20 vision in both eyes but who was functionally blind in one eye — and this a lad who had set his sights on becoming a race car driver!

While direct causal relationships between physical anomalies of the eye and the learning-to-read process have not been established, and while research strongly suggests they never will be, the myth of that connection continues to persevere, often aided by professional groups themselves. For example, some members of the optometric profession years ago hailed eye exercises as a "cure" for reading problems. Although this idea was subsequently discredited, a second generation of optometrists is now touting it. Even among teachers themselves, there is a generally held belief that success in learning to read is dependent upon being able to see well. The persistence of this myth no doubt derives from the cherished belief, mentioned earlier, in the central importance of sight to life itself.

We must also look more specifically at the eye and its place in the physiology of seeing. Inside the eye, on the retina (or back portion) of the eyeball, there are nerve endings called *rods* and *cones*: Cones provide for sharpness of vision, rods gather awareness of light. The rods and cones convert visual stimulation into neural impulses that travel to the occipital lobe located in the back of the brain by way of the optic nerve. What happens to visual stimulation after it reaches the visual center of the occipital lobe is not fully known. It is generally believed that these sensory inputs are dealt with by the brain in a way much like that of a distribution center in which various messages are processed. These individual messages are integrated to provide a coordinated response, part of which is cognitive in nature and part of which is physically related. Some of this processing is involved in reading print, but certainly not all.

There is only one very small portion of the retina that produces the sharpest of vision. That portion, called the *fovea*, is in fact about the size of a pin head. Moreover, the fovea also contains the exit point for the optic nerve (which serves to gather all of the impulses of the retina itself); that point is called the *blind spot* because within it, even the normally sighted are technically blind. The presence of the blind spot can be experienced in a simple experiment: First, on a small card, place an "X" and an "O" on a parallel axis approximately four inches apart. Next, focus with the right eye on the left image, occluding the left eye. By moving the card forward and backward about six inches from the eye, the right target will be seen to disappear and reappear as it moves across the fovea.

The eye will not move smoothly and continuously except when it is tracking the trajectory or other similar movement of an object. As the reader pursues a line of print, the eye consequently moves in short jerks, or saccades, and the reader must therefore maintain focus and bring attention to bear on a new configuration with each saccade. This is true whether one is reading print, a photograph, a landscape, or anything else. As we have learned more about visual processes, some have assumed that the beginning reader needs to be presented with visual targets commensurate with a presumed level of immaturity in the development of eye movements. That children need to be taught with reading matter arranged a certain way on the page is an unwarranted assumption. It would appear, instead, that the necessary visual processes are well in place at a very early age and that instruction directed toward these kinds of skills is unneeded.

The length of time required to register or respond to a visual target has been studied in considerable detail, in part because of great interest in "speed reading," and it appears to be a longer period than one might guess, about a twelfth of a second or so for print. In addition to this, there is the time required for getting from one target to the next, the time in which the saccadic movement occurs. So it can be seen that the direct encounter with print occupies only a part of the time we are "reading." There are consequently real limitations built into reading a line of print, and there are no doubt some important individual physiological differences that determine how fast a person may be able to read a page.

Even among skilled fluent readers, there are further built-in physiological limitations governing the amount of print that can be attended to in any one fixation, or "stop" of the eye. From eighteen or so inches, the approximate distance at which most reading of print takes place, the fovea of the eye is capable of keeping only a few centimeters of print in sufficient focus to secure our attention, and if the target (book) is closer, even less can be apprehended at one fixation; the quantity of print one can perceive at a single fixation is thus a physical limitation with which the reader must cope. Although the distance involved in any particular saccade will vary according to the width of individual targets (i.e., shorter or longer words will influence the reader's response), by and large several fixations and saccades will be required in reading a line in book-size material. One can expect to make about three fixations per line of single-column newsprint, for example. The notion that these can be stretched out is consequently only wishful thinking.

There are, therefore, both physiological and mechanical factors that "speed reading" cannot surmount. Speeding up reading behavior can only consist of increasing the efficiency of what one already does slowly, and in only a limited sense. The most obvious way to increase the amount of material covered is to increase the familiarity of its content for the reader. And so "speed reading" really becomes an activity that goes beyond the "mechanics" of reading (i.e., a fixation followed by a saccade during which the reader attends to a continuous line of print). However, skimming or rapid review is certainly a desirable behavior to encourage. Many readers have developed poor habits as a result of being taught to go from one word to the next, "saying" each word in sequence. The result often is a failure to encompass the two or three words available for "seeing" at any one time. Breaking the "sound barrier of reading," being able to process more than 150 to 175 words per minute (the speed at which average readers function) becomes impossible. Beyond the 500 to 750 words per minute exceptionally fluent readers may manage to process in a conventional manner lies the notion of speed reading (actually, skimming), a misnomer since physical limitations preclude employing the normal saccadic eye movements required in print reading beyond this level of functioning.

Hearing and the Hearing Process

As I have suggested, the ability to hear normally is fundamental to all verbal languaging activity and is far more significant than seeing in making reading behavior possible. As I have also emphasized, one can "read" and still be blind. All that is needed is a set of symbols capable of being a full substitute for print, and that is available to us in Braille. There is no such substitute available where hearing is concerned, unless it is finger spelling. Signing is, as the word implies, something standing in lieu of a full symbol system. The history of the education of the deaf is replete with evidence of the disabling effects of deafness on human intellectual and social development (Furth, 1966; Padden & Humphries, 1988; Scouten, 1984).

Like the eye, the ear "receives" what is basically a physical property itself, sound (in contrast with light), and, assuming hearing is intact, converts it into neural impulses through a series of steps. The first step is the mechanical action upon the eardrum, although the eardrum itself is not actually essential to hearing, as the application of a tuning fork directly to the boney part behind the ear demonstrates, for sound can be perceived directly by the inner ear in this fashion. However, in normal instances, the action upon the eardrum in turn results in a second mechanical action, transmitted through three small hinged bones in the middle ear. These are in turn attached to the cochlea, a spiral-shaped portion of the inner ear containing a fluid that also travels through the semicircular canal just above it, where balance is controlled.

Mechanical movement activated by the sound, which is obviously totally exterior to the ear itself, results in a push-pull effect at the point of connection with the cochlea. This action causes the fluid within the cochlea to produce a wave-like motion that selectively acts upon the hairlike neural endings covering its inner surface. Just how this functions is not clearly understood, but somehow different portions of the cochlea are stimulated and differentiated according to the frequencies and intensity of the particular set of sounds being perceived. Frequency refers to the wavelength, or tone, of the sound. One rarely hears a pure tone, since nothing in nature can be said to produce only a single frequency; as a result, "pure" tones are found only in the laboratory. Intensity has to do with the loudness of the sound. Frequency and intensity interact with individual differences among hearers to produce differences not only in which sounds are available for hearing, but at what intensity they may be heard. Persons with a hearing loss will be unable to hear sounds those with so-called "normal hearing" will hear; other people—the very few with supersensitive hearing (*hypercusia*)— can perceive sounds that people with normal hearing cannot.

The transformation of a physical entity, sound, into a neural impulse is thus completed, and the neural system is ready to relay the transformed message to the various parts of the brain where it will be acted upon *if* appropriate attention allows awareness of it to exist. It is possible to be unaware of a meaningful stimulus even though that stimulation is available for processing. If we are unable or unwilling to allow the awareness necessary to begin processing the stimulus, it will go unnoted, unread.

That we are not prisoners of our nervous system therefore bears emphasis. Just as with the visual process, or any one of the sense modalities capable of delivering a "message," the ability to hear does not mean we are destined to hear a particular sound, or, if we are aware of its existence, to make any use of it. This condition holds true for each of the sense modalities. In hearing, some sounds are blocked from consciousness at the start and are not truly "heard" at all; others may be heard but ignored. We hear selectively, for a number of reasons. We may have on our minds: the book we are reading, the television program that has captured our attention, and so forth. We also hear what we are psychologically prepared to process. For example, Helen Kennedy (1963) has studied aspects of hearing behavior by asking people to write familiar and unfamiliar words presented to them verbally. She found that people will "hear" the familiar word at the expense of its unfamiliar soundalike. Similarly, we learn to hear some sounds and not others in various words (and places). Some of us cannot distinguish between *pen* and *pin*, for instance, or between *Mary, marry,* and *merry* when they are presented out of a comprehensible context. More dramatically, persons from different language groups early on assimilate a sound system that excludes both the reproduction and identification of some sounds common to other languages. So there are many other facts that determine, to a larger extent than we sometimes realize, not only whether we will hear something, but indeed what we hear.

The singular significance of hearing in the formation of language will be discussed in detail in the next chapter. Here we need to remind ourselves that a severe loss of hearing is much more serious than most normally hearing persons realize. That is true at any age, but particularly is it the case when hearing loss is experienced from the earliest years. We should also appreciate that profoundly deaf and severely hearing-impaired people experience special difficulties where language development is concerned when compared with their normally hearing peers.

The Neuro-Motor-Cortical Matrix:
Reading and the Black Box

The function of the sense modalities is thus to convert the various forms of stimulation available into neural impulses that are then transmitted to various parts of the brain for processing. They provide each of us with our own window on the world. Without them, the human would be nothing more than a vegetable, unaware and unknowing of the surroundings. We gain all our experiences through them, and the quality of those experiences is determined by how well we utilize them. It is therefore important to consciously direct their development, to enhance their function. The processing of sensory messages is consequently in large measure the result of a decision to attend to them. Yet we are not completely free in that regard; we are to some degree affected by the culture in which we have gained our experiences or knowledge of the world. Odors and tastes may be judged pleasant or unpleasant, for example, on the basis of cultural values. In the same way, the culture often influences the degree to which a particular sense modality may be valued.

Although our knowledge of what actually happens once a stimulation is converted into a sensory input has advanced greatly over the past several decades, we are still relatively ignorant of its intricacies. We have, of course, learned a great deal in a relatively short period of time. It is hardly a hundred years since Broca claimed to be determining human intelligence by measuring the cranial capacity of skulls from different races, using buckshot as a "standard measure"; in the process, and not incidentally, Broca reinforced cultural prejudices about sex differences, to the disadvantage of the female in all racial groups. At about the same time, phrenology was the rage: the telling of human character-

istics, including intelligence, through an analysis of the particular configuration of one's head. A true believer in phrenology was no less a
figure than Horace Mann himself—but then, astrology has its current
adherents, in government and out.

Where reading behavior is concerned, the greatest attention has
been paid to a phenomenon that has been known for a long time: the so-
called asymmetry of the brain, the fact that the brain itself is divided
into two hemispheres, connected only by a mass of nerve fibers called
the *corpus callosum* (the so-called Great Commissure) and by the optic
nerve, which leads from each eye to each hemisphere's occipital lobe,
where visual stimulation is apparently first processed. With the realization that the halves of the brain are not perfect mirror images of each
other, various theories have developed to explain how this might affect
reading behavior (Gardner, 1978). The most widely hailed over the
years, although the most specious, was Samuel Orton's notion, developed in the 1920s, that the evident tendency of some individuals to
reverse letters and words was due to a failure to "see" (note the emphasis
on the visual apparatus) the word in its proper order. Orton surmised
that a lack of "dominance" of one hemisphere over the other resulted in
perceptual confusion, which in turn led to reading difficulty (see J.
Orton, 1966).

He believed that, particularly in people with left or mixed laterality (in handedness, footedness, or eyedness), words were processed in the
wrong hemisphere, resulting in what he called *strephosymbolia*, or
"twisted symbols." Thus, *c-a-t* would be perceived as *t-a-c* or even
as ‑ט‑ק . Although his theory has since been discredited, his followers
founded the Orton Society, which is still very much alive. In fact it is the
second largest organization (next to the International Reading Association) devoted to the problem of reading. While encompassing a broader
view of the problem of reading than at its founding, it still harbors the
ghost of times past. Even some of the remedial techniques developed
during the heyday of Orton's reign have persisted to the present time.

The idea that different functions take place in different hemispheres, nurtured so effectively by Orton, has had a life of its own,
reappearing from time to time in a different, slightly more sophisticated
guise. In the sixties, for example, Glen Doman and Carl Delacato proposed that laterality could be retrained (assuming that right-hemisphere
dominance only was the normal condition), with a resultant improvement in reading performance. Delacato (1963) wrote a book explaining
their theory of how laterality is established, how it might be diagnosed,
and what kind of treatment might correct anomalies. Doman, for his

part, wrote a book, *Teach Your Baby to Read* (1965), which, more than twenty years later, is still being stocked in paperback stalls.

As neurophysiological research has revealed more about the "specialization" of the hemispheres, more complex notions have been concocted about the effect of hemispheric asymmetry on reading (and other forms of behavior). Presentations at conferences, books, and articles (see, for example, Edwards, 1979; Hunter, 1976), have appeared in such profusion that one observer of the scene was moved to comment: "to put it bluntly, academic hucksters have engaged in a scientific shell game" (Gardner, 1978, p. 27). Lacking the neurophysiological and biological basis for appreciating the complexity of cortical functioning, individuals proposing significant and distinct functions between the two hemispheres simply do not know what they are talking about. Instead of showing one-to-one interconnections, the research is gradually demonstrating something quite different—that the brain functions in a holistic fashion, constantly interacting with its entire self as it goes about its job of thinking and acting. Similarly, it is directing and coordinating a very large series of events, some involving motor control (eye movements of various kinds, body position, hand movements in turning pages, etc.) and others a host of finely tuned cognitive and affective responses.

What we know and don't know about the "black box," then, is that we know a lot, but there is much more yet to learn. The evidence so far strongly suggests that thinking, and consequently reading, is carried out in an integrative, and idiosyncratic context. That is, each person is indeed unique. We are once again going through the lesson of the ages. The discovery of a "truth" or "fact," like the asymmetry of the brain, is always an oversimplification of the reality of that truth or fact. The process of growth toward greater understanding is toward further complexity. If that is true, then we cannot expect to find simple answers in our quest to understand the nature of reading behavior.

Related Readings

Andrews, J. F., & Mason, J. M. (1986). How do deaf children learn about prereading? *Annals of the Deaf, 131*, 210–217.

Brierly, J. (1987). *Give me a child until he is seven: Brain studies and early childhood education.* Philadelphia, PA: Falmer Press.

Chall, J. S., & Mirsky, A. F. (Eds.). *Education and the brain.* National Society for the Study of Education, 77th Yearbook, Part II. Chicago: University of Chicago Press.

Dreby, C. (1979). "Vision" problems and reading disability: A dilemma for the reading specialist. *The Reading Teacher, 32*, 787–795.

Furth, H. G. (1966). *Thinking without language: Psychological implications of deafness*. New York: The Free Press.

Gould, S. J. (1981). *The mismeasure of man*. New York: Norton.

Hart, L. A. (1983). *Human brain and human learning*. London: Longman.

King, C. M., & Quigley, S. P. (1985). *Reading and deafness*. Boston: College Hill Press.

Kolers, P. A. (1969). Reading is only incidentally visual. In K. S. Goodman & J. T. Flemming (Eds.), *Psycholinguistics and the teaching of reading* (pp. 8–16). Newark, DE: International Reading Association.

Mindel, E. D., & Vernon, M. (1987). *They grow in silence*. Boston: College Hill Press.

Padden, C., & Humphries, T. (1988). *Deaf in America: Voices from a culture*. Cambridge, MA: Harvard University Press.

Pickles, J. O. (1982). *An introduction to the physiology of hearing*. New York: Academic Press.

Regan, T. (1985). The deaf as a linguistic minority: Educational considerations. *Harvard Educational Review, 55*, 265–277.

Scouten, E. L. (1984). *Turning points in the education of deaf people*. Danville, IL: Interstate Printers & Publishers.

Springer, S. P., & Deutsch, G. (1981). *Left brain, right brain*. San Francisco: W. H. Freeman.

Taylor, K. K. (1978). People hearing without listening: Problems of auditory processing in the classroom. *Research in the Teaching of English, 12*, 61–76.

CHAPTER 5

Beginnings: Listening, Talking, Thinking

The major developmental task in language learning during the first months of life is to establish a phonological capability for the first, or native, language. But growing apace, and certainly of equal importance, is the budding capacity for thought that commences at least with the first breath and comes to flower much later than does the capacity to use language itself.

Since infants come into the world without language, and since we have tended to equate thought with language rather than considering them quite distinct entities of a very different order, it is not surprising that the early years, and particularly the first year or two, have been thought of as a quiescent, even passive period, certainly not one in which thinking as such might be said to exist. The towering work of Jean Piaget (1898–1980), the Swiss epistemologist/psychologist who has been referred to as "the giant of the nursery," has changed our thinking in this regard in a most dramatic fashion. His contributions to our understanding of how the quality of a child's thought grows and evolves, while no doubt subject to considerable modification as our knowledge base expands, remain monumental. They also give important insights into the interrelationships between thought and language, a fundamental distinction of great importance as we examine language-learning processes in all of their modes. But more of that shortly.

Learning to Talk

Before Speech

The first 9 to 12 months or so of every child's life around the world is spent without any form of usable speech. The emergence of speech is the consequence of growth along two independent but interrelated de-

velopmental lines, both of which have foundations in the inheritance of
the youngster but are more profoundly influenced by personal experiencing. (In the nature-nurture dichotomy, as far as language is concerned, nurture is by far the more important.) One of those developmental lines has to do with the emerging ability to construct the sounds
that correspond with those of the child's speech community well enough
for mutual understanding to become possible. The other has to do with
the child's developing intelligence, in the course of which language will
become a vital tool in the process of re-presenting (representing) remembered experience, an ability central to all that follows. It is not the only
tool available for this purpose; there are, for example, drawing and
writing, along with various dramatic forms. All are means of expressing
ideas past or present. Different cultures find some more valuable than
others. Still, it is characteristic of all children to engage in these ways of
expressing ideas, one which differentiates human behavior from that of
other animals.

The newborn's birth cry marks the beginning of work toward ac-
complishing the first major task in achieving the ability to speak, gaining mastery over the sound system or phonology of the language that the
child will hear and learn to speak. It can safely be presumed that
everyone is born with the potential for speaking *any* language because
the child's learning is in no way dependent upon its race or national
origin. Rather, learning is dependent upon what language the child will
hear in everyday living. And so we may view the first months of life as a
time when the child learns to produce the sounds appropriate to speaking the "first" or native language, with all its warts, contusions, and
variants from the larger speech community of which it is a part. As these
processes continue, in some fashion which we do not yet understand
well, the potential for producing the sounds appropriate to any or all
other languages is cast aside, or at least eclipsed until, perhaps, the time
comes to learn a second language.

Speech Begins

True speech is usually said to begin when the child starts to put two
or more words together to convey a thought. For a majority of children,
this event occurs sometime between the ages of 18 and 24 months.
However, there is obviously a prior period during which the child begins
to develop a vocabulary of single words. We can never be sure when the
beginning point of that development has been reached because its notice
is dependent upon an adult's ability to recognize it, but in most cases,
we see this happening somewhere between 9 and 12 months. Nor can we

be sure of what that first word (or words) will be. Despite our efforts to "teach" a child its "first word," or install specific words subsequently in the vocabulary, that matter stays largely out of control, a lesson about language development and teaching that most adults find difficult to learn. Despite a firmly entrenched belief that language is learned largely by imitation, we now know that it is not.

At the same time, we are not certain just how children do learn to talk. After the "first word," the child acquires a vocabulary of single words, perhaps 75 to 100, before the next stage in language development occurs. No doubt many of these words are learned imitatively; the parent points to a picture, and such words as *doggie, cow, horsie*, and so on are assimilated into the emerging language structure. But the child's world is not taken up completely by nouns, by naming. At the same time, other words for which there are no concrete referents begin to creep in: *mine, please, yes, no*, and the like. Somehow, words describing action, modifiers, even personal-social words are found in the child's vocabulary at this so-called pre-linguistic stage. Just the ability to learn the notion of *my* or *mine* suggests something more than mere naming ability instilled through imitation is happening here.

But when the youngster says *MILK!*, obviously meaning that more is wanted, or *SHOE!*, where the indication clearly is that there is a shoelace requiring tying, we know we are hearing something of a different order. And so what is called *holophrastic speech* provides a sort of bridge between a more simple use for language and something much more complex. In a very short while, the child will, in some fashion, move through a developmental period that makes possible both a vocabulary of several thousand words and the syntactical and grammatical abilities needed to utilize that vocabulary in intelligible speech.

Thinking and Speaking

How Thinking Develops

While the emergence of true speech is a remarkable event in itself, there is an underlying, and more fundamental development, one actually more important than speech alone because it is what makes speech possible. That is the emergence of the ability to *re-present* (or represent) prior experience through symbolic means. Although Piaget made a life-long study of the development of cognitive, or thinking, abilities of children ranging from birth through the adolescent years, the richest data he has left to us have to do with the early years. Until he began his research more than 60 years ago, the popular consensus was that the child's thought processes were qualitatively similar to that of the adult, only immature. That there might be as dramatic a change over time in cognitive characteristics as the one obviously present in physical growth patterns had not occurred to teachers any more than it had to parents. Piaget was to single-handedly change that, although prejudice in the academic community against his research methods delayed publication of his findings in the United States long after they were available in Europe.

While Piaget's discoveries will be modified as research continues into the growth and development of cognition in children, his fundamental assertions remain sound: that the thought processes of the child growing toward maturity are qualitatively different from adult patterns of reasoning, and that, although that development may take idiosyncratic lines, there are general patterns to which all adhere. Piaget identified four major developmental stages, within which he enumerated a number of substages. Figure 5.1 shows the four major stages, the ages at which they begin to emerge, and the cognitive behaviors typical of each as described by Furth (1970/1986, p. 33).

An example of one preoperational substage will serve to illustrate how detailed was Piaget's inquiry into the cognitive developmental process while suggesting the importance of his discoveries to our knowledge of child thought processes. Up until about 4 months of age or so, "out of sight, out of mind" is the rule: If an infant drops a block or other object it is giving its attention to and the object no longer can be seen, attention immediately shifts to something that can be apprehended directly. However, this begins to change; the child achieves what has been termed "object permanence," learning that out of sight is *not* out of mind. In other words, he can now comprehend that the object still exists even though he cannot see it. A further development in this particular substage, then, is developing the ability to play peek-a-boo, a more ad-

Figure 5.1.   The Four Major Developmental Stages Identified by Piaget

Stage	Onset	Typical Activities
Sensorimotor	Birth	Perception, recognition, means-end coordination
Preoperational	1–2 years	Comprehension of functional relations, symbolic play
Concrete operational	6–7 years	Invariant structures of classes, relations, numbers
Formal operations	11–13 years	Propositional and hypothetical thinking

Source: Furth, 1970/1986, p. 33. Reproduced by permission.

vanced stage within the general notion of object permanence. Here is one example of the critical ability to recall experience or to engage in representational thinking. Evidences of this sort illustrate that the child's intellectual growth begins early and continues to evolve, even though no language per se is yet available for use.

It can be seen that Piaget conceptualized a hierarchical ordering of thought processes through which all children progress as they grow from infancy to adulthood. His ideas have put to rest the notion that children are little adults and that the problem in teaching is to "dumb down" tasks that might be appropriate for adult learning to match their relative immaturity. Rather, Piaget showed us that children think in ways that are qualitatively different from those of adults, passing through the several major stages outlined in Figure 5.1, each with several substages, and that teaching should employ procedures compatible with this fact of development. His theory that these stages are more or less finite and irreversible has stirred increasing criticism as too rigid and deterministic. But the basic premise that there are sequential and qualitative changes in thought processes in development remains secure, and the impact of his thinking, although it has yet to be felt in any substantial way in American schools, will eventually be great.

Piaget's concept of stages in the development of thought emerged from his abiding interest in the natural sciences — zoology in particular — and in classifying phenomena (Piaget preferred being called an epistemologist rather than a psychologist, the latter being a field in which he had virtually no formal preparation). He began his work with children as a young scholar largely as a result of an association with Alfred Binet and the Binet Laboratory in Paris, where Binet had written the first successful intelligence test in the early part of the 1900s. Rather than focusing on correct answers (the idea behind testing and assessment as developed in the United States), Piaget became fascinated (as was Binet) with "wrong" answers. That is, he began to explore why children gave the answers they did, right or wrong, but particularly those answers that, though incorrect to adults, seemed perfectly logical to the child. Out of this developed a clinical method of research that provided the basis for his theory and has become widely used here and abroad.

Because Piaget based his research on the reports of very few children, and because he used research techniques held in low regard by psychologists in the United States, relying as he did on clinical observations of children rather than objectively derived scores on tests predetermined to elicit certain kinds of information, his work for many years failed to attract approving attention. The objective test had long since become the sine qua non of educational research in the United States, and anything deviating from it was viewed not only with suspicion, but not infrequently with hostility. In fact, Piaget's first book, *The Language and Thought of the Child*, first published in the late 1920s, did not find a publisher in the United States until the 1950s. Piaget's other books languished as well, although toward the end of his life, his ideas began to gain wider acceptance, and he was increasingly lionized. Most educationists had not even heard of Piaget until the 1960s, and a relatively few can be counted among his readership even today, although many have read *about* him.

The first of Piaget's four major developmental stages in children's thinking, the sensorimotor stage, begins at birth. During this stage, the time during which the child appears to learn almost exclusively through direct sensory stimulation, Piaget identified six substages, each progressively more complex, culminating in the emergence of the preoperational stage, during which representational thinking also becomes possible. (The reader should keep in mind that there are no abrupt points of change along this continuum; it is a gradual process with no dramatic road markers.) The child at the preoperational stage, in contrast with the youngster functioning at the sensorimotor stage in learning, has become able to make something—a word, an object, a mental symbol or image—stand for or represent something that is not being directly apprehended and manipulated.

Clearly, then, the quality of thinking in the preoperational stage is different from its predecessor. Now, instead of being bound by motor operations, by feeling and touching and moving, the child tends to be dependent upon visual perceptual processes, and overwhelmed by them as well. For example, when water is poured from a low, squat beaker into a tall narrow one, the child will likely insist there is more water in the tall beaker because it appears that way. He will be unable to realize that manipulating the shape of the container does not change the quantity of water at all. Piaget devised numerous experiments of this type to illustrate the many variations in this fundamental ability to *conserve*, that is, to mentally reverse actions taken on an object (in the case of the beaker, to mentally reverse the process to verify whether the quantity has indeed changed, or whether something else irrelevant to the initial question is the culprit).

Indeed, the initial question itself may be the culprit in assessing whether *conservation* has been established, and a number of researchers in the more recent past have attempted to determine its role in the discovery of child thought processes. So far the evidence appears to suggest that the nature of the examiner's question, including the kind of tasks required, will alter responses such that, under certain circumstances, children younger than Piaget has suggested may be able to conserve to a greater extent than previously thought. That this applies to other levels of thinking may also be true, but a more important possibility is that the entire range of reasoning competence may extend over a longer developmental period than Piaget originally postulated. Despite these evident theoretic flaws, his experiments uncovered important characteristics of child thought processes never before imagined.

It is toward the end of the sensorimotor stage and the beginning of the preoperational stage that the child acquires what Piaget calls the "schemas" necessary for representational thinking. As in the other major stages of his theory of development, he identifies several substages. Thus, the ability to use signs and symbols in thinking emerges along five fronts, each having its genesis — at least for most children — in development during the crucial period from 18 to 24 months. They do not emerge all at once, nor — except for the first two — in any particular sequence. The important thing to consider is that the ability to think abstractly, to *re-present* experience, comes in several different modes, of which verbal language is one of the later developments. In addition, while they are all part of the same cloth — namely, they allow thinking beyond that involved in direct apprehension — each has a kind of independent life. That is, each continues over the coming years to develop into more complex forms of behavior, more complex modes of representing experience. These substages are (see Piaget & Inhelder, 1969):

1. *Deferred imitation.* The first to develop. Here the child imitates a model he has previously seen. Piaget gives as an example the child who, after seeing a playmate in a temper tantrum, imitates the same scene after the child's departure. It includes any behavior that is imitative/repetitive of a previously observed behavior.
2. *Symbolic play.* Such play is basically pretending rather than imitative or repetitive. The child who "converses" on the play telephone in the fashion of its mother is engaged in symbolic play, as is the child who pretends to sleep, or who plays the part of a favorite animal, television personality, and so forth.
3. *Drawing.* The child begins, during these early stages of preoperational thinking, to use tools of various kinds — pencils, crayons, whatever else is handy — to represent ideas on a flat surface. Such representation may for some time be quite obscure to the adult who does not comprehend the "realism" that the child creates. There have been extensive studies of the development of children's art, and other

forms of drawing, particularly in testing; they demonstrate a univer-
sality of developmental patterns surprising to many adults.

4. *Mental imagery.* Here we refer to the ability to conjure in the mind's
   eye past experiences of various kinds. Mental imagery can be observed in block play and other forms of manipulative activities, e.g.,
   in doing cut-out jig-saw puzzles.

5. *Verbal language.* The beginning of language, Piaget asserts, "permits
   verbal evocation [speaking] of events that are not occurring at the
   time, i.e., talking about things in the past or future" (pp. 53–54).

Because of Piaget's puzzling lack of interest in the arts, he failed to
consider in detail several other ways in which experience can be represented: through the plastic media of clay and other materials, such as
paper and cloth, that can be made to take on new shapes; and through
music, dance, and combinations of these two.

According to Piaget, the third major stage in his grand developmental scheme, called *concrete operations*, emerges when the child
begins to realize that in such experiments as that with the beaker of
water, there is no physical change no matter the appearances. Where
before, for example, a modeling clay ball rolled into a "snake" was said
then to contain more clay, or where coins arranged in rows contained
"more" when a one-to-one comparison was no longer possible because
the examiner had extended the space between the coins in one of the
rows, the child can now no longer be fooled by visual perceptions gained
when irrelevant actions are taken. Like all other stages, the concrete
operational one is composed of several substages; it extends from somewhere around the age of 6 or 7 to 12 or 14 or so. Now the child focuses
on several aspects of a situation simultaneously, is sensitive to transformations, and can reverse the direction of his thinking (Ginsburg &
Opper, 1978, p. 168).

The fourth stage, termed *formal operations*, is characterized by the
child's ability to think in abstract terms, to escape being bound to a
physical reality, and to reason hypothetically. Of all the stages, this has
been researched the least. It has generally been thought that children
begin to enter this stage at about the age of 12; in fact, there are
growing indications that many may either *never* enter into formal operational thinking or at least may not do so until well after their teens.
While many economically disadvantaged youngsters have difficulty reasoning hypothetically in the Piagetian sense, many college students from
advantaged homes seem also to find themselves in the same boat. So the
question arises whether this may be a more or less natural phenomenon,
or whether there are circumstances which contribute to it, or both.

How Speaking Emerges

Once a child's thought processes develop to the point that experience can be recalled and thought about — in other words, once representational thinking takes hold — verbal language proceeds at an incredible speed. Growth in this regard takes place in several dimensions: in acquiring vocabulary; in mastering the syntax of the language (the order in which words are placed in a phrase or sentence); and in learning its grammatical forms. At the same time, the child begins the much longer road to semantic mastery, of employing the meanings of words appropriately. But as we shall see, using words as tools for reasoning is a problem of a different order, and development is much slower. However, to illustrate the rapidity with which the child gains a working knowledge of his first or native language, it is useful to review some of the basic information we now have regarding these developments.

With respect to vocabulary size itself, it is difficult to tell exactly how many words are in a speaker's lexicon at any particular time; except perhaps toward the beginnings of this development, we cannot possibly assess the presence of every known word because their number rapidly becomes so large. The usual research procedure to determine vocabulary size, then, has been to get a sample of part of a vocabulary and then compare it against a known lexicon such as a dictionary provides. Of course, the size of the dictionary will influence the total number of words it is assumed a person knows based on the ratio of the two samples — the one from the individual vocabulary and the one from the dictionary itself. And so we come out with more of a guess than anything else, although it may be a reasonably educated one. Even so, it comes as a surprise to many that careful research over the years has produced figures estimating the average 6-year-old's vocabulary to range from about 2,500 to 25,000 or more words. Taking a middle ground between these two extremes tells us it is usual within a 4-year period (from 2 years to 6 years) for a child, on average, to add eight to nine words per day, Sundays and holidays included! (These figures are for a spoken vocabulary.) Estimates of *understanding vocabulary* (words that are understood in context but which may not be in the child's own speaking vocabulary as yet) cover a similar range of extremes, but in each instance are roughly twice that of the spoken vocabulary, or 5,000 to 50,000 words *by the age of 6.*

Considerable research has now been done on language acquisition itself, on the course of development of both grammar and syntax, as well as semantics, or meaning. When these studies were commenced in earnest, in the 1960s (after the invention of the high-fidelity tape recorder and computer made such studies possible), linguists thought that growth in the first two areas (syntax and grammar) was so phenomenal in the early years that, for all intents and purposes, it could safely be assumed to have been completed by the age of 8 (Joos, 1964). Subsequent studies have shown that such a conclusion was not warranted. Growth in power over the finer syntactical and grammatical aspects of one's first language apparently continues beyond this age period, at least through the elementary school years. Research has yet to give us a full picture of language development in these preadolescent years. What we can probably say with assurance, however, is that while not all language development is completed by age 8, as previously thought, the lion's share of growth *is* completed for the vast majority of children by that age.

One's first language, of course, may not be standard English, the language spoken by most of the American middle class. It will, rather, be the language of the home and immediate neighborhood, with all its errors and blemishes. It may well be standard English, in other words, but it may also include the "he don'ts," "liberries," and "I don't want no's" that characterize variations on standard English. Because so much of the oral language has been learned at such an early age, and practiced so extensively, we can be assured it is fairly indestructible; in fact, it will be very difficult if not impossible to root out those "errors," correct them, and generally clean things up. With all its blemishes, this is the language the classroom teacher will have to work with! If a correction is to occur, the chances are it will come about for reasons other than the provision of formal instruction. Change instead appears to come about more often and with greater permanence as a consequence of an inner awareness that the form or pronunciation does not match the social environment in which the individual wishes to participate, or when there are other highly personal reasons for making a change. There must, in other words, be a personal perception of need, along with an inner desire, before lasting change can occur. Where language is concerned, therefore, the parent or teacher who wishes to bring about improvement is best advised to look not at formal instructional techniques, but at the social setting where those subtle influences may do their work.

The matter of semantics, or meaning, is quite a different kettle of fish. While language in general may not necessarily accurately reflect what anyone is thinking, this is especially true of the thinking of the young child. Children become fluent speakers, in other words, long before they become fluent thinkers. When children use speech in an effort to communicate their thoughts, we must keep in mind that words are particularly unreliable indicators of the thoughts and meanings of a young child. The child may seem to mean one thing when in fact something quite different was intended, and while this often appears to be cute or perhaps even insightful from an adult point of view, we need to remember that this discrepancy is likely to be a persistent problem. Similarly, children do not necessarily interpret adult language as the adult intends, which complicates teaching, particularly direct instruction.

The remarkable growth in language that takes place during the first few years of life has been the subject of much study and speculation, but just how does all this come about and what does it mean for teaching and parenting? We do not know exactly *how* children learn to speak and listen meaningfully, let alone *how* they learn to read and write; we can only draw inferences from our growing knowledge about the course of these developments based on observations of children as they learn to engage in these activities. As we have learned how to observe language growing and developing, much of our previous speculation as to what is actually at work appears to need quite drastic revision. We have been inclined to think that it was all explainable within the relatively simple stimulus-response-reward paradigm, with imitation serving as the primary initial avenue for learning. And indeed, this remains a popular way of viewing the entire problem of language development, including both reading and writing development.

As well, we have thought of each of the so-called language arts in a compartmentalized way; speaking and listening, writing, and reading have been perceived as developing along independent tracks, as common instructional practices in our schools so strongly attest. The idea that these divisions might be made up of whole cloth seems to have escaped our attention.

At first blush, of course, the early acquisition process that results in the development of a vocabulary of single words does suggest that all occurs in the relative security of the S-R context. But a second look, particularly one aided by knowledge gained during the past two decades, tells us otherwise. Language acquisition would be a predictable matter if we could be assured of the effectiveness of teaching with a controlled stimulus. We could, for example, predict the first word, the extent of the single-word vocabulary, and so on, none of which we have been able to do following the S-R paradigm. Nor has its widespread application in reading instruction produced the results it theoretically promises.

I have recounted how the invention of the portable high-fidelity tape recorder made it possible for the first time to catch language "in flight," so to speak, holding it there for intense scrutiny and analysis. Let us now turn to a brief review of the development of this research. One of the first studies was by Ruth Wier (1962), who taped monologues of her 2½-year-old son, Anthony, as he awaited sleep in his crib. She found that Anthony was engaging in an activity with important consequences. He was not talking randomly, as the casual listener might have assumed. Rather, he seemed to be systematically working toward improving his syntactic and semantic abilities. What Wier observed, as her extensive and painstaking research revealed (she had no computer to help her analysis along, as she would today) was nothing less than a self-directed on-going exercise of emerging capabilities in which there appeared to be a consolidation of skill and a moving forward to new uses as the process continued. As George A. Miller, a Harvard psychologist, noted in his introduction to Wier's book reporting her study, he along with others had not been prepared "to encounter a two-year-old boy who — all alone — corrected his own pronunciations, drilled himself on consonant clusters, and practiced substituting his small vocabulary into fixed sentence frames. . . . The gap between this child's reported behavior and all I had been led to expect from the books of Pavlov, Watson, Thorndike, Hull, and other association theorists was more than I knew how to cope with" (p. 15).

A fluke? No. A number of years later, with such research now greatly assisted by computers, we know that Anthony was not all that unusual; other children of the same age engage in similar behavior. Consider the following example of Anthony's speech, in which he is practicing (and playing with) the conjunction *and:*

> you take off all the monkeys
>   and kitties
>   and Phyllis and Humpty Dumpty
>   and monkey and horsie
>   and vacuum cleaner
>   and Fifi
>   and horsie
>   no house
>   and house
>   and house
>   no records
>   and the blue blanket
>   this the blue blanket. (Wier, 1962, p. 111)

What Wier described has turned out to be characteristic behavior in the child who is learning to speak. Compare this example from Robert Hopper's book, *Children's Speech*, as he records 2½-year-old Brian's bathtub soliloquy. Here we see other kinds of repetitions, but the play element, and the practice, are clearly evident (pp. 4–5).

Chim chiminey chiminey
Chim chiminey chiminey
Here come some
I be right there
I want someone to wash me
wiff my wash cloff
washy washy cloth
I got it all full [referring to washcloth,
    which he put in mouth, then spat several times]

No
Well, hard
Chim chiminey chiminey
Chiminey
I love you

With that
At the other page, she can get it
A store
An hour, an' a page
[in falsetto] Honey, can't wash me
No, no, and we let it out
And she doesn't want me to remember you
Washy washy
Oh the bizzin of the bees [alteration of "Big
    Rock Candy Mountain"]
Oh the bizzin of the bees. . . .

We now see it is primarily through the processes of practice and experimentation that language growth occurs. Recent research has called into question the long-held notion that language acquisition is a relatively passive activity in which vocabulary and grammatical and syntactical abilities are quite literally passed on by example. We have tended to think child language reflected on a more or less one-to-one basis what the child heard those with developed speech say — that child language was a mirroring of it all, in which skill evolved as a function of simple maturational processes. Quite the opposite appears to be true. Every language is rule-governed and has built-in constraints. Rather than learning through the establishing of relatively simple associations between words, sounds, and meanings, it would appear that *the heart of learning to speak lies in the child's own efforts to master the rules governing the language he is seeking to use,* learning in the process how to operate within the constraints of syntax and grammar and the customs of semantic expression. The child thus becomes his own best teacher. Through experimentation and by playing with words, a meta-awareness of the deeply rooted rules governing expression gradually becomes available to him, not in any conscious or rational way, but in the utilitarian sense of being functionally available.

It would be incorrect to assume language develops on its own, without reference to adult models. But we know little of exactly how the Anthonys and Brians manage to utilize the language environment that surrounds them as they work their way toward fluent speech. For example, studies show that parents talk to their children in what has been called "motherese" (and "fatherese"), and it is thought this may facilitate child language production. Mothers, and to a lesser extent fathers because there is usually much less verbal interaction between children and their dads, appear to shorten and make more direct their talk to and with their children. It is an intuitive response, unguided by a logical decision to simplify, to remove the chaff from the wheat, so to speak, when they talk with their child. The extent to which motherese affects language development is not known. We only know that most adults, in conversing with very young children, do this to a certain degree. We are sure, at least, that the child growing up in an environment lacking a speech model will not develop language. That is, of course, extremely rare; there are only a very few documented instances in which this is thought to have occurred (Curtiss, 1977; Fromkin et al., 1985; Lane, 1976). Even so, what is happening in the normal course of events remains a mystery. Anthony and his age-cohorts (the 2- to 3-year-old set) are acquiring a vocabulary so rapidly and from such a variety of sources that even their parents are at a loss to explain where many of the words their children know were learned. Even more of a mystery is how syntactical and grammatical rules are acquired. We can observe forms of behavior that shed some light, in particular the process called "overgeneralization," in which the child intuitively applies rules that logic might dictate but are "incorrect" in terms of language itself. For example, the usual growth process in moving from singular to plural usage takes the child from "foot" to "foots" and finally to "feet." There are numerous situations in which this occurs: "goose" to "gooses" to "geese," "throw" to "throwed" to "threw," "find" to "finded" to "found," and so on.

Relationships Between Thought and Language

The relationship of thought and language in the learning-to-read process is in many ways analogous to the view one gets peering down a long, straight stretch of railroad track: two separate rails, linked by a growing number of ties, that appear to grow ever more closely together as the distance increases. And just as it is true that thought and language are as separate as the two rails, so is it also true that, over time as over distance, they appear ever more closely linked by a myriad of interconnections. But one would not want to ride those rails if the wheels of our vehicle were to travel at a different speeds on each of the rails. And so at this point, our analogy begins to break down. For, as we have seen, the child's power over language begins after thought has commenced, and its growth to relative fullness in terms of its power over the syntax and grammar of the native language, reached by the age of 7 or 8, contrasts sharply with the much slower growth rate of cognitive power. Thus one (language) begins later but is relatively complete early on, while the other (thought), the beginnings of which are indeterminately early, continues to develop for many years, into the twenties and probably beyond. Any vehicle traveling such a track would soon be twisted totally out of shape! If thought developed with language's rapidity, children at age 6 or so probably should be given the vote.

Although children are "linguistic geniuses," in the sense that they acquire in a very short time the ability to employ an extraordinarily complex set of language rules and relationships, it is always advisable to appreciate the very great distance that often exists between what is said and what is meant. As we shall see in the next chapter, great gaps may exist between teacher or parent language and the meaning a child gives to it. The reverse may also be the case: Children commonly have vague and even inaccurate ideas of such things as words, sentences, periods, and the like. The child who said "reading is telling stories in your head" expressed, we would like to think, a consciously poetic sentiment. But we can hardly be sure of that, even though children frequently appear to indeed be creative and imaginative users of their native tongue (Chukovsky, 1968).

Studies of language development have naturally led to inquiry into the possible existence of commonalities in this process within societies where there is a mother tongue other than English. This research has revealed a number of developmental similarities across cultures and across languages, which we now refer to as *language universals*. Through these studies we are realizing that, while the surface structure of the world's many languages varies widely from one to another, there are many similarities, not only in the way children think about their world, but in the patterns that characterize learning with respect to such basic aspects as vocabulary development and the acquisition of grammatical rules and syntactical principles.

Implications for Teaching and Learning

There seems little doubt that the great advancement in knowledge about intellectual development in the early years provides a valuable resource for teachers and others who have responsibility for the education of young children. When we combine it with other information regarding growth and development generally, the central importance of the early years becomes very clear. We see now that the years from birth to 12 are extraordinarily active and important years in child development, and in educational potential, years that lay whatever groundwork there may be for success later on. But what does this mean that the school, or the parent, should *do*? Does it mean we should intensify what we are already doing, and do it earlier on, as many have assumed? Or does it call for some reconsideration of basic procedures?

Consider the fact of an evolving intellect in which thinking proceeds through qualitatively different stages at a much slower pace than language facility itself (which also follows similar but not identical developmental patterns in its growth toward fluency). If Piaget and others are anywhere near the mark, as they appear to be, then we *must* engage in some reconsideration of basic procedures. Most American children begin their formal schooling, and are taught to read in formal instructional settings, while they are in transition between preoperational and concrete operational thinking. With the increased attention to teaching reading in kindergartens, which has marked the recent past, formal instruction begins even earlier. This means that the learning-to-read process is being instituted at a time when the child does not reason well logically in the sense concrete operational thinking allows. Thus we must consider in planning for teaching, and in how we deal with our children as parents, whether the tasks we place before the child are ones that are understandable, or whether they require thought patterns and processes that make little or no sense to the child, reasonable as they may seem to adults not privy to the kind of information presented here. It is far from accidental, I believe, that a very large number of countries traditionally delay formal instruction until the child reaches the age of 7, when most children have reached the Piagetian stage of concrete-operational thinking. Traditions evolve as a consequence of much experience with things that yield satisfactory results only when certain conditions are met. Is it possible this particular tradition has come about because, for reasons we may now only be able to begin explaining in an objective fashion, age 7 serves as a watershed year in the intellectual development of children, enabling them to begin engaging in logical thought processes, such as those encountered in most instructional programs, including reading, that form the basis of the curriculum? Still, that is not to say one cannot learn to read at an earlier age. Advancements in communications obviously can broaden the experience base, just as improvements in diet can enhance physical development. But the extent to which changes of this order can be made probably remains modest; there certainly is no reason to suggest taking the kind of radical steps represented by the recent establishment of "academic" preschools, for example.

The problem posed by formal instructional procedures in the teaching of reading and writing, it will begin to come clear in the next chapter, is not necessarily insurmountable. If one tries to teach a child who has few logical reasoning skills by utilizing formal procedures, it seems obvious that problems will follow. Therefore, when instructional procedures are predetermined without a particular learner in mind, it is best to wait for greater mastery of the logic on which such lessons are based to emerge. Children learn to speak and to listen meaningfully without formal instruction, and it is now evident that similar conditions, as Huey pointed out long ago, are present in the development of reading and writing behavior.

Related Readings

Black, J. (1979). Formal and informal means of assessing the communicative competence of kindergarten children. *Research in the Teaching of English, 13*, 49–68.

Brittain, W. L. (1979). *Creativity, art, and the young child.* New York: Macmillan.

Britton, J. (1970). *Language and learning.* London: Penguin.

Chomsky, C. (1972). Stages in language development and reading exposure. *Harvard Educational Review, 42,* 1–33.

Dale, P. S. (1976). *Language development: Function and Structure* (2nd ed.). New York: Holt, Rinehart & Winston.

Dale, P. S., et al. (1977). *Cognitive development in young children.* New York: Brooks-Cole.

Donaldson, M. (1979). *Children's minds.* New York: W. W. Norton.

Donaldson, M., et al. (Eds.). (1983). *Early childhood development and education.* New York: Blackwell.

Durkin, K. (1987). *Language development in the school years.* Cambridge, MA: Brookline Books.

Dyson, A. H. (1986). Transitions and tensions: Interrelationships between the drawing, talking, and dictating of young children. *Research in the Teaching of English, 20,* 379–409.

Edmonds, M. H. (1976). New directions in theories of language acquisition. *Harvard Educational Review, 46,* 175–198.

Evanechko, P., et al. (1974). An investigation of the relationships between children's performance in written language and their reading ability. *Research in the Teaching of English, 8,* 315–326.

Gardner, H. (1978). *Artful scribbles: The significance of children's drawings.* New York: Basic Books.

Gardner, H. (1982). *Art, mind, and brain.* New York: Basic Books.

Glazer, S. M. (1980). *Getting ready to read: Creating readers from birth through six.* Englewood Cliffs, NJ: Prentice-Hall.

Hall, N. (1987). *The emergence of literacy.* Portsmouth, NH: Heineman.

Hall, N. A. (1976). Children's awareness of segmentation in speech and print. *Reading, 10,* 11–19.

Hawkins, F. P. (1986). *The logic of action: Young children at work.* Denver: Colorado Associated University Press.

Hiebert, E. H. (1978). Preschool children's understanding of written language. *Child Development, 49,* 1231–1234.

Hiebert, E. H. (1981). Developmental patterns and interrelationships of preschool children's print awareness. *Reading Research Quarterly, 16,* 236–259.

Jaggar, A., & Smith-Burke, M. T. (1985). *Observing the language learner.* Newark, DE: International Reading Association.

Larrick, N. (1983). *A parent's guide to children's reading* (5th ed.). Philadelphia: Westminster.

Linneman, A. W. (1979). The emergence of conservation concepts: A longitudinal study. *Research in the Teaching of English, 13,* 153–160.

Lomax, R. G., & McGee, L. M. (1987). Young children's concepts about print and reading: Toward a model of word reading acquisition. *Reading Research Quarterly, 22,* 237–256.

Lowenfeld, V., & Brittain, W. L. (1975). *Creative and mental growth* (6th ed.). New York: Macmillan.

Martin, A. (1985). Back to kindergarten basics. *Harvard Educational Review, 55,* 318–320.

McCarthy. L. (1977). A child learns the alphabet. *Visible Language, 11,* 271–284.

McNeill, D. (1970). The development of language. In P. H. Mussen (Ed.), *Carmichael's manual of child psychology* (3rd ed.; pp. 1061–1161). New York: Wiley.

Opie, I., & Opie, P. (1959). *The lore and language of schoolchildren.* Oxford: Oxford University Press.

Painter, C. (1984). *Into the mother tongue: A case study in early language.* London: F. Pinter.

Parker, R. P., & Davis, F. A. (Eds.). (1983). *Developing literacy: Young children's use of language.* Newark, DE: International Reading Association.

Payton, S. (1984). *Developing awareness of print: A young child's first steps towards literacy.* Birmingham: Educational Review.

Quigley, S. P., & Paul, P. V. (1984). *Reading and language.* Boston: College Hill Press.

Tizard, B., & Hughes, M. (1984). *Young children learning: Talking and thinking at home and school.* Danbury, CT: Fontana Paperbacks.

Wadsworth, B. J. (1978). *Piaget for the classroom teacher.* New York: Longman.

Wadsworth, B. J. (1984). *Piaget's theory of cognitive and affective development.* New York: Longman.

CHAPTER 6

Learning to Read
In School and Out

For many years, it was common practice for teachers, particularly kindergarten and first-grade teachers, to advise parents not to become involved in teaching their children to read. Reading instruction was seen as school business exclusively, and it would be taken care of when the child entered the first grade. Kindergarten, parents were told, was where their child would learn "how to get along with others," a necessary prerequisite to surviving in the more directed environment of the first grade, where children would for the first time need to become serious about learning.

Those days, now behind us, were a mixed bag. On the one hand, we are now quite well aware that many 4- and 5-year-olds can begin on the road to literacy, and we can provide for that possibility, if it is kept in harmony with such other developmental needs as socialization, which remains an important concern at this age. On the other hand, we live in an age of great anxiety about the quality of our schools and mistrust of their ability to achieve their primary purpose. Schools have responded by initiating formal instruction in reading in the kindergarten, where it had been outlawed since the beginning of the kindergarten movement in the United States just after the Civil War. Parents have taken it upon themselves to purchase "how-to-do-it" books — easily found, among other places, on racks scattered about the local supermarket and drugstore — so they can teach their children at home. Preschools and daycare centers, having felt the pressure from parents, now frequently include formal instruction in reading in their curriculums. "Academic preschools" are burgeoning as parents seek ways to avoid what they perceive to be the inadequacies of the public school curriculum.

The trend over the past quarter of a century, then, has been to intensify the formal teaching of reading while extending instruction downward (and upward, as it turns out, since college-level reading instruction is now more the rule than the exception). It is ironic that this has been our response, for during the same period, avenues of communication have multiplied many times over. Young children are today exposed to print in every aspect of their environment, and, as a consequence, virtually every child coming to school for the first time is aware of print, uses it meaningfully in everyday life, and can write his or her own name. Our ignoring the presence of this ability may derive from the same blindness that afflicts those who argue over when language actually begins. Although we may have put away the idea that only teachers should be allowed to teach the child to read, we have *not* given up on the idea that every child only really learns to read as a consequence of direct instruction. And so we have set out what we think each child should be taught, and ignored what they have already learned and what we could base our teaching on. As it is, we base it on nothing; we behave as if the 5- or 6-year-old mind is a *tabula rasa* that can only be written upon by an adult intent upon teaching reading.

Reading and Writing Before School

For one reason or another, relatively little interest has so far been expressed in studying early readers and writers, a sharp contrast with the great interest shown in preschool oral language development. Dolores Durkin has been an outstanding exception to this trend; she has done two extensive studies of early readers (1966), and has followed her original subjects for several years (1974–1975). Most of what else we have available are reports about individual children, often by proud parents who are also professional educationists or psychologists; few of these reports escape the bias that parenthood so often bestows. There are also a number of "how-to" books for parents, books that seem to justify their existence primarily by capitalizing upon the anxiety that besets so many parents about whether their child will master the "mystery" of reading.

In Durkin's research, however, we find valuable insights into some of the conditions that seem to engender early reading (1966). She conducted two similar studies, one at the University of California at Berkeley, and the other while she was a faculty member at New York University; she has also conducted a number of follow-up studies of her subjects. Durkin's basic procedure has been to administer a rather simple test to first graders to determine if they can "read" ("say back") a number of common words. This rough screening has then been followed by the administration of standardized, or "norm-referenced," paper-and-pencil tests, comparing the resulting scores with those obtained from a large number of children who have previously taken the same tests. After the initial screening of several hundred children, 49 were selected for the west-coast study, and 156 for the east-coast study.

Durkin found that, while the intelligence quotient for both groups as a whole was above average (particularly for the New York group, for unexplained reasons), there were children from across the normal range of intelligence: The scores ranged from an I.Q. of 90 on up. This suggests that high intelligence as measured on a standardized test is not necessarily a condition for early reading. The obverse is also true: An intelligence quotient in the low-normal range is not a predictor of backwardness in learning to read. The letter reproduced in Figure 6.1 was written by an early reader who was tested and judged to be considerably below average in the kind of intelligence measured by standardized tests.

Durkin also found that the children in both studies demonstrated a curiosity about words early on, asking questions such as: "What does *that* say?" "How do you write . . . ?" They also copied words and repeated them. She also found that an unusually large number of the children had older brothers and sisters who helped them by answering

FIGURE 6.1. Letter Written by a Child During Her Second Month in First Grade

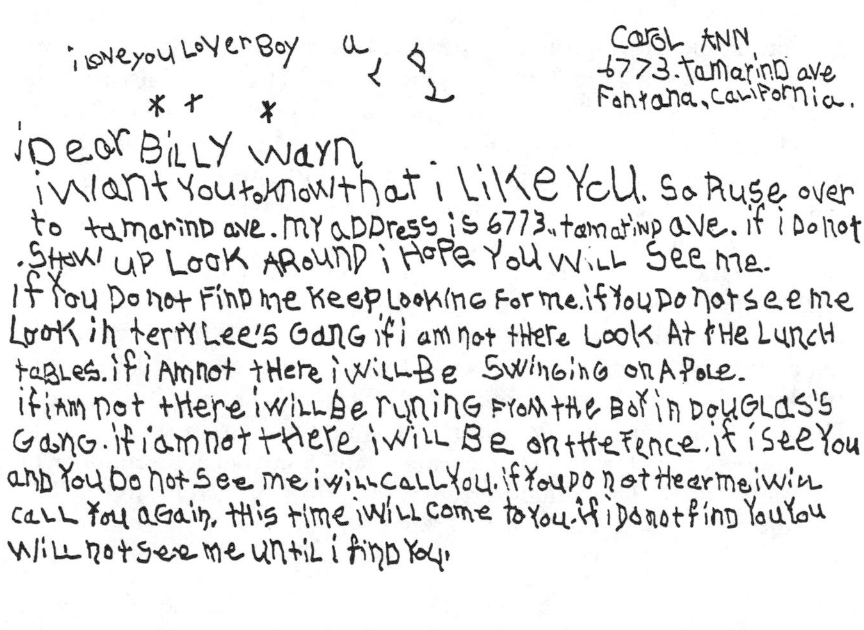
i love you Lover Boy

Carol Ann
6773. tamarinD ave
Fontana, California.

Dear Billy wayn
i want you to know that i like you. So Ruse over to tamarinD ave. my aDDress is 6773. tamarinD ave. if i Do not Show up Look around i hope you will See me. if you Do not Find me keep Looking for me. if you Do not see me Look in terry Lee's Gang if i am not there Look At the Lunch tables. if i Am not there i will Be Swinging on A Pole. if i am not there i will Be runing from the Boy in Douglas's Gang. if i am not there i will Be on the Fence. if i see You and You do not see me i will call You. if You Do not Hear me i will call You again. this time i will come to You. if i Do not find You You will not see me until i find You.

questions, by showing them how to write a letter or word as requested, by responding to whatever it was they wanted or needed to know as they pursued their curiosity about reading print. As teachers, the older children tended to simply answer the question; they did not seek to teach around or to it, or to anticipate what they thought the child wanted or needed to know. Parent behavior followed the same general pattern. In other words, there was no "teaching" as we normally think of it, just "as needed" answers to the child's questions, which of course *is* "teaching," perhaps in the best sense of that word.

Finally, many of the children seemed to get into reading through writing. That is, they first wanted to write the letters and words; after that, they picked up on the idea that writing appeared elsewhere in their environment and could be "read." A related and not surprising discovery was that a sizable number of the children had slates and paper available where their "writing" could be practiced.

In follow-up studies, Durkin reports that earlier starts are not likely to cause reading problems later on, and that early readers tend to lead non-early readers in reading achievement, although this superiority was not consistently observed. One problem for early readers in maintaining the edge they enjoy at the beginning of their reading career is that early instruction may not take into account their advanced ability. Often they appear to be taught as if they were no different from their non-reading compatriots (Durkin, 1974–1975). Though early readers generally maintain their position relative to other children, they are often subjected to instruction that ignores their already existing capacities — an all-too-frequent occurrence — and they therefore do less well, relatively speaking, than they would with teachers who adjusted instruction to their capabilities.

A more recent study of early readers by Arleen Armantage (1986) confirms Durkin's finding of a wide range of intelligence quotient scores among early readers, although the average scores of such a group doubtless exceed the mean I.Q. score of 100.

These studies also demonstrate that there are relatively few children who become fluent readers before the age of 5, since both researchers had to scour the countryside in order to find their subjects. We can be reasonably sure that, although intelligence plays a positive role in the development of reading and writing abilities, its role is minor. Put another way, although some very bright children will become fluent readers prior to their entry in school, many equally bright youngsters will take their time beginning on the road to literacy. Individuals differ so widely in this regard that we do children a grave disservice by equating reading acquisition with intelligence.

A second thing we can learn from studies of early readers concerns the reciprocity of writing and reading. Just as listening and speaking are interdependent, a similar (if not identical) symbiotic relationship exists between reading and writing. We therefore need to think about what this means in regard to both classroom teaching and to parenting. We may be seriously handicapping the possibilities of development where reading is concerned if we divorce it from writing — a common event in most of our classrooms.

Finally, the *lack* of a significant relationship between intelligence and either early reading or the acquisition of fluent reading at any age suggests the presence of a wide range of individual differences in the learning-to-read process. Many years ago, Arthur I. Gates (1937) studied the optimum age for beginning formal reading instruction in schools. It was out of this research that the word was passed as gospel (because Gates was then the most respected reading researcher in the country) that a child should have reached the age of 6.5 (educationese for six-and-one-half years) before being taught to read. That was not the interpretation Gates intended, however. In an article full of caveats, he concluded that instruction in reading begun when the child was $6^1/2$ gave the best odds for the majority of children in the formal learning-to-read process. Warning his audience that his data provided predictive information only with respect to children as a group, he emphasized that it could not be applied to individuals. But his audience didn't listen, preferring to think that Gates' research legitimized a strange notion called "reading readiness," the idea that children pass through a stage of "getting ready" to read, during which time instruction should be directed toward enhancing "readiness" for the formal instruction that was to begin, we were told, at 6.5 years. With that, teachers were advised of ways deliberately designed to teach children skills that were associated with reading but didn't involve words as such. To go along with this, instructional materials were devised for teacher and pupil use; even standardized tests were developed to assess not how ready for instruction a child might be, but how successful the child might be when it was begun. The idea still lurks in the term "pre-reading." We persist in the notion that, in the teaching of reading, there are highly specific items that need to be learned before "reading" can begin: eye movements, configurational or word-outline distinctions that must be distinguished from one another, awareness of similarities and differences between letter-like figures requiring development, and so forth. Whether one will believe this depends on his or her definition of reading. Virtually all of the readiness tasks that have been devised are visually based and as a consequence are derived from that familiar view of reading that emphasizes the visual over the auditory and form (or skill) over function (or meaning).

When Children Come to School

In some two-thirds of the United States, children first enroll in the public educational system between the ages of 4 years 9 months and 5 years 9 months. Youngsters living in those few states not providing public kindergartens enter a year later. Failure to support public kindergartens has generally been decried because the socializing experiences provided in this "year before real school," it has been thought, provide a base for later success. The truth of that assertion has now to be challenged because of the changes which have occurred in the kindergarten curriculum over the past several years.

The traditional kindergarten provided an environment true to the origins of its name, a *kinder,* or child's, *garten,* or garden, an environment in which the children first venture outside of the home for an extended period of time to interact with children from homes different, to one degree or another, from their own. The idea of the kindergarten took shape in Europe during the Enlightenment and came into being under the guidance of the early childhood educators Frederick Froebel (1782–1852) in Germany, and Johann Pestalozzi (1746–1827) in Switzerland. It coincided with the historical discovery of childhood itself, a stage of growth not recognized before the Enlightenment. Jean Jacques Rousseau (1712–1778), author of *Emile,* doubtless had the greatest influence on the early development of the idea of childhood during this period (Postman, 1982). However, the underlying ideas of the kindergarten did not reach American shores until well into the 1800s; the first public kindergartens did not appear until the 1870s. The American kindergarten is thus a legacy of the progressive era.

The traditional kindergarten had as its primary objectives the general health of children and their socialization into the school community; it was to provide the transition between home and school. However, it also came to be a kind of protective wall between the home and the formal school curriculum children encountered when they entered the first grade. Kindergarten teachers were taught to be child-centered rather than subject-centered in their work, and before long, such barriers as the forbidding of the teaching of reading, mentioned earlier, were constructed. Much of this was to come tumbling down as anxious parents, legislators, and the public generally raised their voices to complain about poor reading performance and the apparent failure of children to learn computational skills. And so today, the traditional kindergarten curriculum is, in most cases, heavily concerned with previously banned subject matter. The incursion of subject matter and more formal teaching methods into the kindergarten has not stopped there, since, as I have already mentioned, many nursery schools and child-care programs are, more and more, including formal instructional practices designed to teach children to read and compute, perhaps another manifestation of "the disappearance of childhood" Postman (1982) has written so eloquently about.

We have also seen, however, that today's child comes to school largely in command of the grammar and syntax of a first language, a substantial speaking vocabulary, and an even larger understanding vocabulary. That child has also developed remarkably in cognitive ability, although the road to mature thought remains a rather long one. As we have seen, most children are in fact coming to kindergarten and first grade with the ability to write their own names; moreover, they are also aware of the print world about them and have a beginning understanding of the purpose of print, using it in their daily lives to satisfy needs of various kinds. Would that we could make use of all that learning and knowledge to continue helping them build each of their verbal language abilities!

How Children Think About Reading

Children need to develop a number of concepts about language in order to become fluent readers of print. By far the most important is the one suggested by the child quoted in my opening sentence: "Reading is telling stories in your head." That is, the child must acquire a sense of the purpose of reading, one which makes possible the understanding that there is a reason for engaging in this process, that reason being the making of meanings. If reading is not perceived as a meaningful activity, the child has no reason for engaging in it.

As we have seen, the growth of thinking changes qualitatively over time, beginning with thought governed — even overwhelmed — by direct sensory experiencing or motoric actions (the sensorimotor stage), and moving gradually to thinking with abstractions. We therefore cannot expect the child to use logic in developing an understanding of the purpose of reading. To explain in adult terms the importance of reading will get us nowhere, except perhaps a parroting back of that logic (heard all too often in elementary schools when children are asked why it is important to be able to read). Rather, the idea is built slowly, through the experience of knowing and learning to love books. Parents can have everything to do with establishing this concept by the simple means of reading to the child from the wealth of children's literature available in any library. It is a long process, requiring the devotion of a great deal of time on demand and on a day-to-day, even an hour-to-hour, basis.

The teacher cannot expect children to come to school having this background, but the meaningfulness of reading can be reinforced through school experiences with books and illustrations, no matter how well developed or rudimentary the idea may be in the child's mind. And that goal is accomplished in a similar fashion: by reading regularly (on a daily basis) in the classroom. The "every day" maxim applies to all elementary school teachers, and in my opinion should extend into the grades beyond, especially wherever we find students who have yet to perceive the basic meaningfulness of reading. It should come as no surprise that junior and senior high school students who read poorly tend not to understand the purpose of reading; they view it as a mechanical activity, disassociated from the oral language they speak and understand, over which they have failed to gain mastery because it has never made any sense to them. And it should be equally unsurprising that such students get a great deal of enjoyment (as well as benefit) from being read to.

Virtually every classroom in the United States (probably 98%) puts its primary emphasis in teaching reading upon the so-called "basal reader." This means that most children will be introduced to print reading through more or less formal instructional techniques in which knowledge about letters and words, how they are arranged on the page, and so forth, will be presented as subject matter to be learned. Mastery over that subject matter is generally verified through question-and-answer routines initiated by the teacher working with children in groups formed on the basis of their apparent ability to learn it. While we might wish there would be an option to initiate the teaching of reading through an experiential rather than a subject-matter approach, the reality is that textbook-based instruction remains *the* dominant mode for teaching. Consider what this means for students.

In presenting material in a subject-matter setting, the teacher employs what might be called a "language of instruction." It is one with special terms, knowledge of which is essential to understanding what is expected of the learner. For example, the teacher will ask the child to "sound out" "letters," ask what a "letter" says. She or he will expect children to "find the word that says . . . ," or "tell what the first sound in the word is," and so on. The purpose of periods, commas, capital letters, and the like will be explained, with the intention that the pupils will appreciate their role in language. The range of the "language of instruction" is wide, merging into the world of writing and spelling (but more of that later).

To what extent can we be sanguine about a child's ability to utilize these verbal clues in a meaningful way? Probably to little or no extent, if the research into the nature of children's understandings of the technical language commonly used in instruction is accurate. Some have suspected the presence of a major problem here for a long time. For example, Magdelon Vernon (1957), in an important book on "backward readers" (the British term for children who have trouble in learning to read), concluded that most reading problems stem from what she termed "cognitive confusion," which, in turn, seemed to derive mainly from a failure to understand what was being asked.

To understand what a child is thinking, verbal questions are next to useless. Piaget showed us long ago that young children, through the age of 6 or 7, or even older, harbor the notion that their mind is an open book to adults. They believe grown-ups know what they are thinking and, when questioned, generally try to give the answer they expect the adult wants to hear. That is why studies attempting to probe childhood thinking about reading and learning to read have resulted in adult-like responses — "reading is something you like to do," "it's saying words in the textbook." It is, to them, simply what they are learning to do, and their descriptions are all product-oriented talk, absent of references to meaning. Questions or tasks revealing children's understanding of the learning-to-read process necessarily must be indirect, eliciting their ideas in an inferential rather than a direct way.

Studies, particularly those of Downing (1968, 1969, 1970, 1971–1972, 1973–1974) and Reid (1966), have been most fruitful in leading us to a better understanding of how children really think about reading. Indeed, what they have found is truly eye-opening. For example, it appears that large numbers of children upon entry into the first grade have vague and inadequate concepts of what constitutes a spoken "word." In one study children up through the age of 8 confused isolated phonemes as well as syllables as "words" (Downing, 1973–1974). It has been found not at all unusual, as well, for notions of the length of "words" to cause confusion when children try to decide whether a word qualifies as such. Single letters, for example, even "a" and "I" are simply *not* words, and two-letter words may also be rejected as such. It has also been found that children tend to divide long words, to combine short words (to make a "word"), and to use "tall" letters as boundaries in determining whether the definition is properly met or not.

As children grow in their understanding of what constitutes a word boundary, in their comprehending the purpose that spaces between words serve, they have been observed to pass through five stages before reaching a sufficiently complete definition (Downing, 1970):

1. Letters can be words.
2. A word is a unit made up of more than one letter.
3. Spaces are used as boundaries unless the words are short; in that instance, they are put together or combined, but when long, they are divided.
4. Only long words are divided.
5. Spaces indicate word boundaries except where there is a "tall" letter in the middle of a word.

It has also been discovered that young children have little understanding of the purpose and content of books. It is not uncommon for children at this age to deny that books contain stories, for example. As well, they confuse drawing with writing, and they may believe any human utterance constitutes a "word." They frequently confuse terms such as *numbers* and *letters*, *more* and *less*, *before* and *after*, *first* and *second* (or *last*), *above* and *below*, *top* and *bottom*, *middle*, *beginning*, and *end*, or *ending*. As well, they do not comprehend what is meant by a "sound" (of a letter), or what it means to "sound out." The confusion is furthered by having trouble in understanding what a "part" of a word might be. Young children are obviously going to be handicapped if they have hazy or inaccurate understandings of what the teacher is talking about when the reading lesson gets under way. And parents can easily reinforce the confusion by adopting a similar vocabulary when they try to help the child.

There can be little doubt that the data indicate 6-year-olds have great difficulty with the concepts entailed by the language employed in traditional instruction. Even a cursory glance at the typical teacher's manual for any of the currently used reading textbooks will reveal how widespread is the use of such terminology in everyday classroom life and how heavily this must weigh on children who are attempting to learn. Think how confused a youngster could become if his teacher were to talk about beginning and ending sounds, letters and words, where the middle of something is, or where something begins or ends. Even finding the bottom or the top of a page may present a confusing command! Never mind that there is, or should be, a story to be told.

How *does* a youngster learn that "reading is telling stories in your head"? Words are of course *not* concepts, although it sometimes seems as if we were only too willing to ignore this distinction, assuming that saying is knowing. Words can only *stand for* concepts, which in turn stand for a cluster of ideas we apply to a specific situation. Understanding that there is a beginning or an ending of a word requires an awareness of beginnings and endings. These are truly complex ideas. And while we may drill a child until a word is remembered, at least for a time in a specific situation, that does not mean the word and its concept are connected in any meaningful way. Lev Vygotsky, a brilliant Russian psychologist who was a contemporary of Piaget until his untimely death in the early 1930s, put it succinctly more than fifty years ago:

> Direct teaching of concepts is impossible and fruitless. A teacher who tries to do this usually accomplishes nothing but empty verbalism, a parrot-like repetition of words by the child, simulating knowledge of the corresponding concepts but actually covering up a vacuum. (1962, p. 83)

The concepts entailed in traditional approaches to reading instruction can be learned, it becomes clear, only by inference, as a consequence of a number of different kinds of related experiences. This is patently true of all concept learning. We call upon words, and other ways of representing experience, to communicate our own particular ideas (or concepts) about something. But without the *experience*, concepts remain empty and meaningless.

Concepts Basic to Reading

Traditional or subject-matter approaches to the teaching of reading obviously entail using a "language of instruction" that common sense tells us needs to be understood if the child is to benefit from this kind of teaching. Some have urged that direct teaching of concepts used in instruction be undertaken, in the belief it will result in the child acquiring knowledge of that special vocabulary (Johns, 1972). But as Vygotsky warned, such an approach may perpetuate rather than solve the problem. The more reasonable route would seem to be to seek ways in which instructional terminology would simply not be used until a later time, *when experience has provided children with an understanding of concepts commonly associated with descriptions about how attention can be called, in a shorthand way, to portions of a text.*

Reading print *can*, of course, be learned without reference to the specific vocabulary of instruction. Durkin's studies (1966, 1974–1975, 1978–1979) of early readers, and everyday experience with children who learn through an experiential approach, attest to the needlessness of this vocabulary. In these instances, children do not attempt first to master the mechanics of print. Instead, they first ask questions about meaning. Pragmatic questions about form follow. In other words, from the very beginning, *form follows function.* Questions under these circumstances serve to clarify experience and make new applications of it possible.

Learning to read thus is akin to learning to swim in that there are only one or two really basic concepts requiring mastery; skill develops as a byproduct of *doing*, rather than by attempting mastery through any conscious, detailed knowledge of the activity itself. In swimming, for example, there are two concepts basic to mastery: (1) discovering that it is possible both to put one's head in water and to coordinate breathing at the same time, and (2) learning that putting one's head in water makes it possible to float. When the two are present, swimming becomes possible. The teacher/coach of swimming knows how fundamental these two ideas and the accompanying abilities are to all that comes later. Without one or the other, swimming cannot occur, so there must be great care at the start to see that such learning is positive and constructive in nature. After that, the teacher/coach's job is one of helping the swimmer refine pre-existing capabilities.

Coaching, or teaching, does not consist of transferring knowledge from the knower to the learner; direct transfer of knowledge is an impossibility. Rather, it consists of knowing what the desired behavior consists of and providing guided practice toward that end. In this view, the learner must engage in the process in order to refine skill. Guidance is given only to the extent it may enhance abilities as they currently exist, and it is therefore stingily and cautiously provided. Thus it is that the learner/swimmer largely learns through self-instruction. Central to it all, of course, is the fact that to engage in practice, one must have a desire to continue it. There must be a payoff for the individual; what the coach/teacher gets out of it is ultimately peripheral. Without the student's desire, the result will remain at best desultory; the behavior will be forced and will only occur in the presence of one who can invoke it through enforcement.

I believe the analogy with print reading and writing is a very close one. In these behaviors there are, similarly, a very few basic concepts the child must develop before mastery can be achieved. First, and most importantly, the child must have an understanding of the *meaning of reading.* The "telling stories in your head" definition of our 5-year-old suggests he was well along in achieving this understanding. Just how he arrived at this definition we cannot be sure, although it undoubtedly

arose as a result of his understanding a number of concepts about reading itself. But being able to give a definition of reading, particularly
when it is so charmingly put, while nice, is not essential. One need not
define something in order to *know* it. Tacit knowing is powerful in its
own right.

In any event, an understanding of the meaning of reading is the
cornerstone upon which all will be built. This overarching perception or
understanding consists of numerous concepts about language, all acquired largely by indirection, as a consequence of a variety of experiences. Some of them have to do with language itself: that there is such a
thing as "language"; that it consists of discrete words (initially, the child
apparently perceives of it to be a series of connected sounds); that these
spoken words can be written down; and that they "say" the same thing
time and time again, and so forth. Others have to do with books themselves: that they are made up of many strings of printed words and stir
interesting and pleasureful ideas in our heads; that they contain stories
that can be repeated over and over again. These ideas cannot be taught
directly; they can only be developed by repeated exposure in settings
that promote interest and attention.

Thinking and Reading

A confounding problem for children in the beginning stages of
learning to read is suggested in Piaget's construct regarding cognitive
development itself, not just in the emergence of concepts regarding the
nature and purpose of language, important as that may be. As I have
suggested, reading instruction in its usual form makes demands on children's cognitive capacities that do not appear to fit their reasoning
abilities. The reader will recall the brief discussion in Chapter 5 of child
thought during the preoperational and concrete operational periods.
Many children have not achieved concrete operational thought when
either "readiness" or initial reading instruction is begun. Yet the intellectual tasks they are expected to perform while they complete assignments
related to their reading lessons appear to demand that level of thinking
if they are to be completed meaningfully. Some elaboration of the differences between preoperational and concrete-operational thinking will
illustrate this potential dilemma.

As we have seen, the child at the preoperational stage — that stage
in development during which direct perception (seeing, feeling something) overwhelms logical deduction — either is unable or finds it difficult to "make transformations." In Chapter 5 I described the classic

instance of the two beakers with equal amounts of water being perceived as having different amounts according to the height of the water in the narrower beaker — the usual preoperational response. The child at the concrete-operational stage immediately sees through the ruse. Similarly, where an equal number of coins is laid out in two rows, with a greater distance between coins in one of those rows, the child at the preoperational stage will perceive the row covering the greater distance as having more coins. Similarly, when shown equal amounts of modeling clay rolled in two balls that are then made into "snakes" of different thickness, the child selects the thinner and consequently longer one as containing more clay. In each of these instances we have an example of thinking that is directed by appearances despite the logic of knowing that equal amounts of material had been "transformed." Piaget, his followers, and his critics have devised many experiments to explore the depth and range of sensorimotor or preoperational thinking (as well as the nature of what has now been termed *concrete thinking*, the next major stage in development). That some aspects of this kind of reasoning may be present earlier, as some assert, still does not change the likelihood that this *type* of reasoning can have an effect on children's learning. Consider the following examples of conservation-type instructional practices commonly observed in classrooms. In a phonics-based methodology, lessons requiring the substitution of initial (and sometimes medial and terminal) letters are presented as exercises in word identification (-*at* is to be manipulated as *c*at, *f*at, *s*at, *r*at, etc.). In a whole-word-based methodology a common demand on children's thought processes is to find words within words. In both instances, children are asked to manipulate print mentally, playing a game in which new formulations result through an abstracting process. They are being asked to imagine actions of substitution we would not expect of a child who has yet to become "concrete-operational" in his or her thinking.

The relationship between cognitive development and learning to read has been studied, although to a limited extent. Jenkins (1978) found, in a study of 5- to 9-year-olds, for example, that those children who were clearly at the concrete-operational stage had become independent readers. However, with only a few exceptions, those children who were "preoperational" in their thinking had still not achieved independence in reading print. For the children who were apparently in transition between preoperational and concrete-operational thinking — those who were beginning to do one or two conservation tasks successfully — some were reading independently, and some were not. Jenkins' research reports more clear-cut results than some others of this type, although the suggestion of a connection is present in a number of other studies (see, for example, Kolls, 1980). If it is subsequently proven that there is a relationship between the quality of child thought and learning to read, how is it that some very young children become fluent readers well before the time we might expect them to have achieved concrete-operational thinking? One possibility is that print reading has not been denied to these children. In other words, it may simply be that the conditions for learning affect the child's opportunity to utilize print effectively, and that instruction based on procedures requiring thought processes beyond the present reach of the child's intellect may discourage or even delay reading development.

Piagetian theory sees age 7, the time when it is believed the concrete-operational stage is fairly well established, as a kind of watershed year. Indeed, as I have noted earlier, it is traditional in many cultures to consider that age as a time when indications of maturity are first perceived. It has also been the modal age for beginning reading instruction in countries around the world, the traditional time for beginning one's formal education.

Piaget's description of the course of cognitive development adds a new dimension to the old issue of which method teachers should use in the classroom. That argument has been long-standing one. Although we have been singularly unsuccessful in finding a clear answer to that issue, the most notable failure to find the "one best method" is without a doubt to be found in the Cooperative Reading Studies sponsored by the Department of Health, Education, and Welfare between 1964 and 1968 (Bond & Dykstra, 1967). Twenty-seven studies were set up in first grade classrooms around the country to test the hypothesis that some methods, perhaps even one method, of teaching children to read would be clearly superior to others. At the end of the first research year, no statistically significant differences appeared. Still optimistic such differences would reveal themselves, the research was continued through the second grade with 13 of the most promising of the original research dyads. A similar finding of no difference appeared at the end of the second year. Ten of the remaining research projects were continued through the third grade. At the end of that time, sufficiently clear findings had still not appeared, and the effort was abandoned.

In a further analysis (Lohnes & Gray, 1972), the authors pointed out that a substantial portion of the findings of these studies were associated with one factor, what they termed general intellectual development, further confounding the findings (which, all told, cost $1,660,395 in 1969 dollars). In other words, they believed that tests of reading achievement tested abilities similar to those measured on a group intelligence test. It seems evident reading test scores deluded the original researchers into believing reading to be a finite ability capable of being assessed with some precision.

After expending so much effort on the search for a "best method," with such discouraging results, it is perhaps understandable, if not logical, to find reading experts shifting the blame for the reading problem from the "method" to the teacher. And this is what happened after the dust had settled on the Cooperative Reading Studies, even though they did not include a direct assessment of this aspect of the problem of learning to read. While the importance of a good teacher cannot be discounted, neither can the "fit" between the reader and the learning circumstance be put aside cavalierly. Those who would shift the responsibility to the teacher have failed to consider the possibility that both whole-word and phonics (code-emphasis) instructional programs may indeed differ in only minor ways from one another. If that is the case, as I have argued, the findings of the Cooperative Reading Studies might have been anticipated. If they had, perhaps the focus of the research would have shifted to the meaning vs. structure, the *evoke-invoke* dichotomy.

Related Readings

Allen, R. V. (1965). *Attitudes and the art of teaching reading*. Washington, DC: National Education Association.

Allen, R. V. (1966). Bring your own: An invitation to all children to bring their personal language to school. In M. P. Douglass (Ed.), *Claremont Reading Conference, 30th Yearbook* (pp. 25–32). Claremont, CA: The Claremont Graduate School.

Allen, R. V. (1973). *Reading programs: Alternatives for improvement*. Washington, DC: American Association for Elementary-Kindergarten-Nursery Educators.

Allen, R. V., & Allen, C. (1976). *Language experience activities*. Boston, MA: Houghton Mifflin.

Anderson, G. S. (1984). *A whole language approach to reading*. New York: University Press of America.

Armantage, A. A. (1986). *Reassessing the implications of Piaget's theory for reading instruction: A comparison of the cognitive and art development of early readers of print and their yet-to-read peers*. Unpublished doctoral dissertation, The Claremont Graduate School, Claremont, CA.

Ashton-Warner, S. (1963). *Teacher*. New York: Simon & Schuster.

Baghban, M. (1984). *Our daughter learns to read and write: A case study from birth to three*. Newark, DE: International Reading Association.

Barbe, W. (1961). *An educator's guide to personalized reading instruction.* Englewood Cliffs, NJ: Prentice-Hall.

Beck, I. L., et al. (1981). Basal readers' purpose for story reading: Smoothly paving the road or setting up a detour? *Elementary School Journal, 81,* 156–162.

Braun, C., & Froese, V. (Eds.). (1977). *Experience-based approach to language and reading.* University Park, MD: University Park Press.

Brogan, P., & Fox, L. K. (1961). *Helping children read: A practical approach to individualized reading.* New York: Holt, Rinehart & Winston.

Burke, E. M. (1986). *Early childhood literature: For love of child and book.* Needham Heights, MA: Allyn & Bacon.

Butler, A., & Turbill, J. (1984). *Toward a reading-writing classroom.* New South Wales: Primary English Teaching Association.

Chomsky, C. (1970). Reading, writing, and phonology. *Harvard Educational Review, 40,* 287–309.

Chomsky, C. (1971). Write first, read later. *Childhood Education, 47,* 296–299.

Chomsky, C. (1979). Approaching reading through invented spelling. In L. B. Resnick & P. A. Weaver (Eds.), *Theory and practice of early reading* (Vol. 2, pp. 43–65). Hillsdale, NJ: Lawrence Erlbaum Associates.

Clark, M. M. (1976). *Young fluent readers.* London: Heinemann Educational Books.

Clay, M. M. (1982). *Observing young readers.* Auckland, NZ: Heinemann Educational Books.

Corcoran, G. B. (1976). *Language experience for nursery and kindergarten years.* Itasca, IL: F. E. Peacock.

Denny, T., & Weintraub, S. (1963). Exploring first graders' concepts of reading. *The Reading Teacher, 16,* 363–365.

Denny, T., & Weintraub, S. (1966). First graders' responses to three questions about reading. *Elementary School Journal, 66,* 441–448.

Duker, S. (1971). *Individualized reading.* Springfield, IL: Charles C. Thomas.

Dunne, H. W. (1972). *The art of teaching reading: A language and self-concept approach.* Columbus, OH: Charles E. Merrill.

Durkin, D. (1978–1979). What classroom observations reveal about reading comprehension instruction. *Reading Research Quarterly, 14,* 481–533.

Emery, D. C. (1975). *Teach your preschooler to read.* New York: Simon & Schuster.

Fader, D. N. (1968). *Hooked on books.* Berkeley, CA: Medallion Books.

Ferriero, E., & Teberosky, A. (1982). *Literacy before schooling.* Portsmouth, NH: Heinemann Educational Books.

Fields, M. V., & Lee, D. (1987) . *Lets begin reading right: A developmental approach to beginning literacy.* Columbus, OH: Charles E. Merrill.

Francis, H. (1973). Children's experience of reading and notions of units of language. *British Journal of Educational Psychology, 43,* 17–23.

George, M. Y. (1970). *Language art: An idea book.* New York: Chandler.

Glasser, W. (1986). *Control theory in the classroom.* New York: Harper & Row.

Goodall, M. (1984). Can four-year-olds "read" words in the environment? *The Reading Teacher, 37,* 478–482.

Goodman, K. S., & Goodman, Y. M. (1977). Learning about psycholinguistic processes by analyzing oral reading. *Harvard Educational Review, 47,* 317–333.

Goodman, K. S., et al. (1987). *Language and thinking in school: A whole-language curriculum* (3d ed.). New York: Richard C. Owen.

Greenberg, J. C. (1982). *The language arts handbook: A total communication approach.* University Park, MD: University Park Press.

Hall, M. A. (1981). *Teaching reading as a language experience* (3rd ed.). Columbus, OH: Charles E. Merrill.

Hancock, J., & Hill, S. (Eds.). (1987). *Literature-based reading programs at work.* Melbourne, Australia: Australian Reading Association.

Herrick, V. E., & Nerbovig, M. (1964). *Using experience charts with children.* Columbus, OH: Charles E. Merrill.

Hiebert, E. H. (1978). Preschool children's understanding of written language. *Child Development, 49,* 1231–1234.

Hiebert, E. H. (1984). A developmental sequence in preschool children's acquisition of reading readiness skills and print awareness concepts. *Journal of Applied Developmental Psychology, 5,* 115–126.

Huck, C. (1987). *Children's literature in the elementary school.* New York: Holt, Rinehart & Winston.

Johns, J. (1980). First graders' concepts about print. *Reading Research Quarterly, 15,* 529–549.

Kane, F. (1982). Thinking, drawing, writing, reading. *Childhood Education, 58,* 292–297.

King, C. M., & Quigley, S. P. (1985). *Reading and deafness.* Boston: College Hill Press.

King, E. M., & Friesen, D. T. (1972). Children who read in kindergarten. *Alberta Journal of Educational Research, 18,* 147–161.

Kohl, H. (1973). *Reading: How to.* New York: Dutton.

Kohl, H. (1976). *On teaching.* New York: Schocken.

Kohl, H. (1984). *Growing minds: On becoming a teacher.* New York: Harper & Row.

Krashen, S. D. (1985). *Inquiries and insights: Essays on language teaching, bilingual education, and literacy.* Hayward, CA: Alemany Press.

Larrick, N. (1983). *A teacher's guide to children's books* (5th ed.). Philadelphia: Westminster.

McCarthy, L. (1977). A child learns the alphabet. *Visible Language, 11,* 271–284.

McCracken, R. A. (1972). *Reading is only the tiger's tale: A Language arts program.* San Rafael, CA: Leswing Press.

MacKay, D., & Thompson, B. (1970). *Breakthrough to literacy.* London: Longman.

Mason, G. (1967). Preschoolers' concept of reading. *The Reading Teacher, 21,* 130–132.

Mason, J. M. (1980). When do children begin to read: An exploration of four-year-old children's letter and word reading competencies. *Reading Research Quarterly, 15,* 203–227.

Meek, M. (1983). *Achieving literacy: Longitudinal studies of adolescents learning to read.* London: Routledge & Kegan Paul.

Minovi, R. (1976). *Early reading and writing: The foundations of literacy.* London: Allen University.

Nagy, W. E., et al. (1987). Learning word meanings from context during normal reading. *American Educational Research Journal, 24,* 237–270.

Neville, M. H. (1982). *Towards independent reading.* London: Heinemann Educational Books.

Pappas, C. C., & Brown, E. (1987). Learning to read by reading: Learning how to extend the functional potential of language. *Research in the Teaching of English, 21,* 160–177.

Povey, G., & Fryer, J. (1972). *Personalized reading.* North Hollywood, CA: International Center for Educational Development.

Reid, J. F. (1974). *Breakthrough in action: An independent evaluation of "Breakthrough to Literacy."* London: Longman.

Resnick, L. B., & Weaver, P. A. (Eds.). (1979). *Theory and practice of early reading* (2 vols.). Hillsdale, NJ: Lawrence Erlbaum Associates.

Soderberg, R. (1977). *Reading in early childhood: A linguistic study of a preschool child's gradual acquisition of reading ability.* Washington, DC: Georgetown University Press.

Stauffer, R. G. (1970). *The language-experience approach to the teaching of reading.* New York: Harper & Row.

Steinberg, D. D., & Steinberg, M. T. (1975). Reading before speaking. *Visible Language, 9,* 197–224.

Stine, S. (1980). Beginning reading — naturally. In M. P. Douglass (Ed.), *Claremont Reading Conference, 44th Yearbook* (pp. 144–155). Claremont, CA: The Claremont Graduate School.

Taschow, H. G. (1985). *Cultivation of reading: Teaching in a language/communication context.* New York: Teachers College Press.

Taylor, D. (1983). *Family literacy: Young children learn to read and write.* London: Heineman Educational Books.

Teale, W. H. (1980). *Early reading: An annotated bibliography.* Newark, DE: International Reading Association.

Teale, W. H. (1984). Reading to your children: Its significance for literary development. In H. Goelman, A. A. Oberg, & F. Smith (Eds.), *Awakening to literacy* (pp. 110–121). Exeter, NH: Heinemann.

Teale, W. H. (1986). The beginning of reading and writing: Written language development during the preschool and kindergarten years. In M. Sampson (Ed.), *The pursuit of literacy: Early reading and writing.* Dubuque, IA: Kendall/Hunt.

Templeton, S., & Spivey, E. M. (1980). The concept of "word" in young children as a function of level of cognitive development. *Research in the Teaching of English, 14,* 265–278.

Trelease, J. (1987). *The read-aloud handbook.* New York: Penguin Books.

Veatch, J. (1965). *Individualizing your reading program* (rev. ed.). New York: Putnams.

Veatch, J. (1972). *How to teach reading with children's books* (3rd ed.). New York: Citation Press.

Weiss, M. J., & Hagen, R. (1988). A key to literacy: Kindergartner's awareness of the functions of print. *The Reading Teacher, 41,* 574–578.

West, R. (1967). *Individualized reading instruction: Its implications for the teacher and librarian.* Port Washington, NY: Kennikat Press.

Whitehead, R. (1968). *Children's literature: Strategies of teaching.* Englewood Cliffs, NJ: Prentice-Hall.

Yadon, D., & Templeton, S. (Eds.). (1986). *Metalinguistic awareness and beginning literacy: Conceptualizing what it means to read and write.* Portsmouth, NH: Heinemann Educational Books.

CHAPTER 7

Writing, Spelling

We have seen that speaking and listening emerge simultaneously, although in patterns unique to each child. And despite the variations in vocabulary and deviations in the developmental course where matters of grammar and syntax are concerned, the oral language learning process remains very much an interactive one in which each is dependent upon the other for development to occur. Although practice contradicts the prospect that a similar, if not quite identical, interrelationship pertains between writing and reading, we are increasingly becoming aware of its existence. After honing our research skills on oral language development — listening remains elusive because of our inability to halt it long enough to conduct analyses of a similar sort — we now have the tools with which to examine writing development in a similar kind of detail. The period since the 1970s has, as a consequence, been rich in producing new information about the emergence of writing, although the interaction I write of has been recognized for a much longer time. Roach Van Allen has been the most articulate in this regard since, beginning in the 1950s, he has advocated what he has termed "the language experience approach," in which writing and reading are intimately interrelated from the very beginning. Allen's (1961)thesis is contained in the following:

> What I can think about I can talk about.
> What I can talk about can be expressed in
>   writing (in drawing, or some other
>   form of writing).
> Anything I can write I can read.
> I can read what I write and what other
>   people write for me to read. (p. 60)

Tradition Will Out

The conventional approach, where it has been de rigueur to teach writing and reading separately, has obviously contrasted sharply with Allen's language experience approach, what I have been terming an *experiential* or *naturalistic* approach to language development. In traditional practice, as well, we have preceded instruction in writing with that designed to produce the ability to read print. Later, normally in the second grade, instruction commences that is designed to teach the child to write. The teaching of writing in most instances thus rests on a formalistic base. That is, the child is expected first to learn how to produce individual letters (with the expectation that letter names have already been learned). Beyond that, the first stages of writing more often than not require copywork, frequently re-recording a sentence or two written on the chalkboard by the teacher. The writing may be an arbitrary selection of the teacher, or perhaps something selected, but edited, in the fashion of a cooperative story. Writing one's own ideas is generally perceived to be an appropriate classroom activity *after* the physical skill of recording letters correctly and the ability to transcribe models of "correct" writing have been established.

It has been widely acknowledged that traditional approaches to writing instruction have borne little fruit, and there is currently, and quite independently of the reading curriculum, a revolution in writing instruction now going on in the United States. Although it is unsafe to claim that any innovation in education is totally new — all the curriculum permutations observable throughout the history of American education, at least since the latter part of the nineteenth century, in one way or another can be traced to a prior similar attempt at reform — there are unique aspects to the current situation. One is the recognition being given to the idea that teachers who do not write well are hardly equipped to teach others to write and that it may therefore be necessary to provide for the re-education of teachers. A second is that writing improvement results primarily from *practice:* One learns to write mainly through the experience of writing.

Although there have been numerous efforts launched to improve the writing abilities of students, particularly at the secondary level, I know of none which has developed so quickly and spread so widely as the one which began as the Bay Area Writing Project at the University of California (UC) at Berkeley, in the late 1970s. It began as a program to help high school teachers become more effective in their classrooms through first teaching the teachers with the expectation that they would then replicate their experiences with their students in the classroom. The idea spread, first to other campuses in the UC system, and then to other universities as they sought to improve the writing of their own students. So rapid was this growth that in a few short years on the Los Angeles campus of UC, for example, the writing programs staff of 100 offered 360 sections of writing classes to over 7,400 students (Hartzog, 1984).

The "writing revolution," stimulated in a major way by the Bay Area Writing Project, has now spread across the country and is known as the National Writing Project. Specialists in the teaching of writing have found appointments on most university faculties, and altogether the effort represents one of the most successful curriculum development efforts ever to gain a foothold in American education. However, it needs to be pointed out that much of what has happened so far has to a large extent been motivated by a need to remediate what has been perceived as a growing problem among high school and college students. Although the ideas behind these writing projects have begun to affect elementary school curriculums, they have not found the fertile ground that the remedial needs of older students provided. The traditional notions of the learning-to-write process, focusing on skill development and "correctness" in rendering words to the page, continue to predominate. We are still intolerant of "error," especially when there yet appears time to teach the mechanics of writing, and are fearful of a public that is quick to criticize the teacher of young children who fails to demand correctness in their writing.

Writing Beginnings

I have mentioned how research into oral language development has given us the kinds of research tools we need to begin understanding the beginnings of writing, and, concomitantly, of the ability to write employing the usual conventions of *correct* orthography. I believe one of the major problems in teaching writing derives from what seems to me an overweening insistence on *correctness* at every stage of development. Although societies differ regarding the onus they place on the inability to spell accurately or write clearly — in England, for example, teachers and parents are much more forgiving — Americans are only too well aware of the negative light in which such sins are viewed on this side of the Atlantic. As a consequence, we design instruction in writing so it will be fail-safe; in the process, we preclude early attempts at expressing ideas or feelings or refuse to recognize them for what they are, or we seek to correct these efforts, to *teach* the proper form, ignoring the intent of the young writer.

Why do we do this? I can only assume it is because of our great fear that kids of all ages will never be able to *correct* their mistakes if someone else doesn't command it of them. If we have any leads from oral language learning, of course, we should know by now that our chances of truly correcting the writing of others are slim indeed. And we should know that delaying opportunities to write is as unfair as it would be if we demanded correctness in early speech, denying as best we could the chance of a child talking until attempts at speech were completely correct. One of the first studies to reveal the role of writing in reading, and of the unimportance of correctness in written expression at the early stages of learning to write and to read was done by Carol Chomsky in a piece called "Write first, read later" (1971). She reports in a case study format her experience with a 4-year-old as he experimented with writing (and learning to spell). Chomsky suggested that there appeared to be patterns of development in writing much like those being discovered in the development of speech. Since then, researchers have plumbed that hypothesis, finding that, indeed, we can see patterns in both writing and spelling development highly similar to those observed in the development of oral language.

One of the first developments in children's writing is the appearance of the ability to make representations for their own name. That development is now so universal, it is safe to say most children entering kindergarten are able to express their being by recording, with sufficient accuracy so an adult can recognize it as such, the letters that "stand for" their persona. Children growing up in an environment that encourages exploration with pencil or crayon will try to express their ideas in a more comprehensive fashion.

Yetta Goodman (1980) has explored writing development during these early years. She notes that "it has been obvious that many children write their own name to represent themselves, to label their possessions, drawings or dictations or to sign a letter or card for a family member or friend as early as three years" (p. 18). This development quickly gives way, if the conditions are ripe for it, to other kinds of writing activity. Giving examples, she cites Suzie, at age 4, creating a note of words and symbols to remind herself to put the silver tongue of her shoe buckle in the fourth hole in her sandal so it wouldn't be too tight (see Figure 7.1a). Another 4-year-old wrote a note to his mother to let her know "I'm going to be outside" (see Figure 7.1b).

FIGURE 7.1. Early Writing: Notes of Two 4-Year-Olds

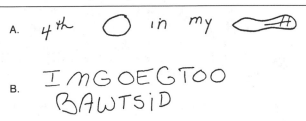

Cathy DuCharme, as part of her doctoral studies, has collected numerous samples of the writing of children of different ages. In Figure 7.2, the two examples of kindergartners' efforts to express their thoughts illustrate how children of similar ages find themselves at different developmental levels. By comparing the work of a 6-year-old in Figure 7.3, we can see the wide variation that occurs between this age group and 5-year-olds.

Once again, if we can observe such development in an environment unfettered by "instruction," yet rich enough in experiential opportunities and materials useful in writing (pencils, crayons, paint, paper, tables, chairs, floorspace, etc.), we will see certain behaviors emerging quite spontaneously. These will begin to be evident after the oral language has been firmly established, sometime within the ages of 3 and 4.

One of the first things children apparently discover is that they are living in a world of signs and symbols. Clearly, the child's perception of that world is immature, incomplete, unfinished in its development. At the earlier stages, it appears that children perceive what we would term writing as drawing. They begin quite literally to draw letters, and as in the earlier stages of language development, a great deal of spontaneous repetition appears as pencil or crayon begin to be wielded. Doubtless, the most common development that the adult is able to perceive as a complete effort to write is when the child masters the writing of his or her name. At that stage, it appears the child is still creating signs rather than actually writing; the written name quite literally *stands for*, or is a *sign for* the persona.

Leading up to this remarkable accomplishment, we observe in children's drawings representations of figures and objects, but also of forms, the origins of which are much less clear. In the process, the child grows toward increasing muscular control while beginning to gain mastery of the skills needed in representing the letters of the alphabet. As these early squiggles begin to take recognizable form, we see various deviations which, again in our zeal to label apparent visual perceptual aberrations as pathological, continue to set off bells of alarm. We see, for example, reversals of letters, even inversions, and of course "spellings" that are often beyond our ken to decipher. The mixture of signs with symbols (i.e., *real* writing) continues for some time, at least into the 6th year and sometimes beyond. Still, in virtually every instance, the process appears to bear a close similarity to grammatical and syntactical development in the oral language: There is a gradual, idiosyncratic growth toward competence in representing the conventions of written language.

Basic to it all is the understanding that "print talks," as our young

FIGURE 7.2. Kindergartners' Writing Samples

The dinosaur
was walking
and eating.

One day it was my Dad's birthday
and we were outside with balloons
and we let the balloons go.

Source: DuCharme, 1987, pp. 172-173.

FIGURE 7.3.   A 6-Year-Old's Writing

Hapey Brthday to my Mom
Hapey Brthday to my Mom
Hapey Brthday to my
Mom!!!!!!!!!!!!!!!!!!!!!!!!
Hapey Brthday to!!
my Mom!!!!!!!!!!!!!

Source: DuCharme, 1987, p. 169.

man's definition informs us when he said that "Reading is telling stories in your head." That idea, combined with the growing ability to form letters *and* the realization that groups of letters form things that we can *say* through writing, makes a more mature form of writing possible. However, a very large number of "errors" appear in such writing as the child discovers the meaning of punctuation marks, capital letters, spacings between words, and the various other nuances of writing that make it intelligible and meaningful. The poem in Figure 7.4, by an 8-year-old, illustrates the possibilities in writing development and the rapidity with which that can occur (DuCharme, 1987).

It is abundantly clear that children who have an opportunity to write will do so spontaneously, that they thoroughly enjoy writing, getting great personal satisfaction from this activity. It also seems clear that, in the very beginning stages of learning-to-write, the child repre-

FIGURE 7.4.   An 8-Year-Old's Poem

My Dream For the World

"My dream for the world (If I had my way)

"Would make the world arise to quite a diffrent day,"

" There would not be hunger under the sun,

" And as for wars I'd proclaim there would be none,

" It would be the door to happiness my freinds,

" And as for sorrow it would be the end.

by Jeremy

MY DREAM FOR THE WORLD

"My dream for the world (If I had my way)"
"Would make the world arise to quite a different day."
"There would not be hunger under the sun,
"And as for wars I'd proclaim there would be none,
"It would be the door to happiness my freinds,
"And as for sorrow it would be the end.

by Jeremy

Source: DuCharme, 1987, p. 175.

sents thoughts with signs, gradually coming to appreciate the distinction between signs and symbols, at which point growth toward mature writing increases rapidly. We can speculate on the significance of the period preceding the emergence of fluent writing. My judgment is that we have underestimated the importance of these early writing efforts to the emergence of fluent reading and writing and that we should consequently arrange environments that encourage this behavior with more care.

Learning to Spell

Inherent in learning to write is the question of how the child acquires the spelling conventions of his native language. Recall (from Chapter 2) that Noam Chomsky and others have described the concepts of "surface structure" and "deep structure." The former refers to the *apparent* arrangement of the constituent parts of a language. We can describe the surface structure through studying the sound patterns of the spoken language or through the ways those sounds are arranged in written or printed discourse. Deep structure refers to the meanings language, in either form, represents. Until relatively recently, analyses of oral and written language have emphasized the surface structure, out of which the popular notion has grown that English, particularly, is rife with exceptions, leading to the assumption that learning to write required gaining mastery not only over the "regularities" but of the many "irregularities" evident in the language. Where learning to spell is concerned, therefore, it was assumed that one could only master the conventions of spelling by learning the rules governing those words that conformed to them, *and*, in addition, by memorizing those that did not. For many years, as a result, we have sought to teach children to spell in isolation from writing, and to teach mastery over individual words primarily through memorization. Along with that, the rules of spelling (e.g., *i* before *e* except after *c*, except as in "neighbor" and "weigh") were to be taught in the hope that knowledge of such rules would make possible the correct spelling of other words without directed attention at learning them through conventional methods.

For as long as teachers have been concerned about the spelling of their students, frustration over the lack of transfer from the process of studying how to spell correctly to spelling in the "real world" has been self-evident. A pupil who receives a perfect score on the weekly spelling test often comes a cropper when attempting to write the same words in a communicative context. Moreover, although the rules of spelling may have been taught with zeal, application of those rules to new situations occurs rarely, if ever. Indeed, it appears that such rules, whether they are intended to help students "unlock" the sounds of the letters in a word (thus presumably allowing recognition and the development of meaning) or assist them in spelling a word correctly, can be applied only after the horse is out of the barn. That is, children appear to be able to apply rules in such instances only when the word is already known to the reader or writer (see Burmeister, 1968; Clymer, 1963; Emans, 1967; Rosso & Emans, 1981; Tovey, 1980).

Despite the monumental evidence at hand to every teacher who seeks to teach "spelling," we nonetheless persist in the notion that "correct" spelling can only be taught in an associationist environment, expecting that each word spelled correctly must be learned as such on an individual basis. To that end, for example, the federal government has supported large-scale research into identifying the degree of regularity found in commonly used words, with the intention of using the findings as a guide in preparing spelling textbooks (see Hanna et al., 1966). And noted figures, such as George Bernard Shaw, have railed against the seeming arbitrariness of English and advocated various schemes to simplify the spelling; Shaw adopted some simplified spellings and bequeathed a portion of his estate to research in this area. At least since the mid-1800s, various such plans have been put forth, the most notable one in recent years by Sir Robert Pittman, who for a time bankrolled the Initial Teaching Alphabet (I.T.A.), a 44-letter substitute for our 26-letter alphabet designed to gain a closer correspondence between phoneme and grapheme (sound and letter). Even Melville Dewey, creator of the Dewey Decimal System so widely used in libraries, became caught up with the idea, writing his paean to its glory in an extended essay published in the opening portions of his catalog of categories librarians use to classify the books on their shelves.

Since the early 1970s, evidence has been accumulating showing that older conceptions of how children learn to spell, with their concomitant methods of instruction, are totally inadequate. Advancements in our analytic skills learned from earlier research into oral language development, as I have pointed out, have provided us a base for studying spelling development. Learning to spell, like learning to talk and to write, is a creative, rule-governed process that proceeds through a series of steps, or stages. And as is the case for speaking and writing, growth in spelling follows a generally similar path but is also idiosyncratic. Depending upon such varied factors as personal experiencing, environmental opportunity, and individual differences generally (intellectual, social, emotional), the young child makes generalizations about "spelling," over-generalizes those rules, and then modifies them in a continuous process of finding the appropriate rule-governed behavior.

While our understanding of spelling development is far from complete, and while, as in learning to speak and to listen, we are not at all certain *how* such learning occurs, we appear to be gaining an accurate picture of the broad outlines of the learning-to-spell process. In the beginning stages, for example, when seemingly undirected scribbling begins to take on a definite form, we note that though written forms vary from one language community to another (e.g., Arabic, English), certain internal consistencies are evident. As in the early stages of learning to speak, the characteristics of the first language, whether spoken or written, begin to be practiced, and those useful in another language fall to the wayside (Y. Goodman, 1980). As development progresses, the child forms hypotheses about the ways in which the oral language may be rendered in its written form. These are tacit hypotheses; that is, they are not consciously known. They are, as well, what we might call "working hypotheses," notions tested out through writing, initially grossly inadequate from an adult point of view, but constantly revised as awareness of convention slowly emerges.

In the beginning, it is not surprising to discover that children misspell virtually all of the words they attempt to write. Although they can identify and know the letters of the alphabet and relate them to the sounds of words, when they attempt to write words themselves, they produce what can only be called *invented spellings* (Hodges, 1981, 1982). That is, they begin by writing the letters whose names sound like those sounds, e.g., *fas* for *face*, *bk* for *book*, *lade* for *lady*. The writings of first graders in Figure 7.5 provide other examples of this phenomenon (DuCharme, 1987).

By studying free writing situations, researchers have identified three apparently invariant stages of development (Hodges, 1981):

1. The children used letter-name strategies much in the same fashion as Read (1971) had observed.
2. They refined the first stage, particularly where vowel sounds were concerned, and began to use letters standing for sounds *other than* those which stood directly for the letter sounds themselves.
3. They began to make direct use of information about the English writing system, e.g., they wrote *gaet* for *gate*, *biek* for *bike*.

In a further study by Beers et al. (1977), 200 children in first grade were asked to spell two lists of words, one of which was familiar, the other unfamiliar. As might be expected from Helen Kennedy's research, familiar words were more likely to be spelled correctly. However, unfamiliar words were not only more often misspelled, it was discovered that in their misspellings, the children tended to revert to the earlier stages described above. When they were not able to spell the word, for exam-

FIGURE 7.5. Sample Writings of First-Graders

A. A first-grade boy writes of a recent trip to San Francisco

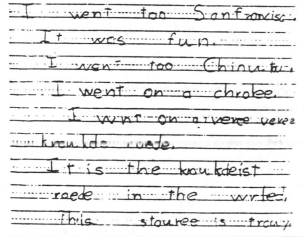

I went too San Francisc.
It was fun.
I want too Chinutown.
I went on a chrolee.
I wnt on a vere veree
    kroukde roede.
It is the kroukdeist
    roede in the wrled.
This stouree is trauy.

I went to San Francisco.
It was fun.
I went to Chinatown
I went on a trolley.
I went on a very very
    crooked road.
It is the crookedest
    road in the world.
This story is true.

B. A 6-year-old girl invents a jingle

Five litle strsts
Sat dawnd no mrs
a loy cam a moon
and sat dawnd
and say a toon
and fitint the strsts
    uwa

Five little stars
Sat down on Mars
Along came a moon
And sat down
And sang a tune
And frightened the stars
    away!

C. A first grader writes his own fairy tale after a class discussion about fairy tales

Once apant a time there where three
hnters. they only celd sheep and cows
and pigs. they celd the sheep and the
cows because you can make heve gakits
and the pig to eat. one day they where
hnting and they saw a manster. the
manster ea eat them aaaaaaaaam!!!!!

Once upon a time there were three
hunters. They only killed sheep and cows
and pigs. They killed the sheep and cows
because you can make heavy jackets
and the pig to eat. One day they were
hunting and they saw a monster. The
monster ate them. Aaaaaaaaaam!

Source: DuCharme, 1987, pp. 171, 175.

ple, they would revert to assigning letters to words on the basis of letter names.

Subsequent work, particularly that of Henderson, has led to the hypothesis that there are five such stages in spelling development (the last stage being the "correct" one). He described these five stages as follows (1985, p. 144):

1. *Preliterate* (ages 1–7)
   Scribbles
   Identifies pictures
   Draws
   Imitates writing
   Learns letters
2. *Letter Names* (ages 5–9)
   Most sight words spelled correctly
   Invented spelling by letter name
3. *Within Word Pattern* (ages 6–12)
   Most sight words spelled correctly
   Invented spellings honor short vowels and long vowel
      markers
4. *Syllable Juncture* (ages 8–18)
   Sight words may or *may not* be transferred to spelling
      performance
   Invented-spelling errors occur at juncture and schwa
      positions
5. *Derivational Consistencies* (ages 10–100)
   Sight words may or *may not* transfer
   Invented spellings "most frequently misspelled"

Since spelling research is still relatively incomplete, there is much yet to learn. What we can say with considerable assurance from what we do have at hand is that children begin writing with perceptions about the relationships of sounds to symbols quite different from their mature, "correct," or acceptable form. As I have pointed out previously, it would appear children begin on the road to writing by employing signs, even when those signs take the form of letters and even words (e.g., the child's own name) familiar to the adult. They will, for example, gladly engage in "pretend writing" in which squiggles that appear as meaningless marks will be "read back" in a similar fashion each time (as long as they are accompanied by a drawing that represents the experience of the youngster). But even when there begins to be a conscious attempt to relate letter sounds to the sounds as they occur in words, the child perceives a reality different from that of the adult. As Richard Hodges (1983) points out to us,

> Learning to spell is a complex intellectual accomplishment. The available evidence potently demonstrates that a rich linguistic environment is not only essential in the development of oral language but in the development of written competence as well. Every interaction with written language both in and out of the school setting affords an opportunity to gain new information about the structure and uses of the written code. Only in a very limited sense is knowledge of the writing system learned as an outgrowth of words that are individually memorized in spelling class. (p. 41)

Reading, Writing, Spelling, and Thinking:
Some Thoughts in Retrospect

We have seen once more in this as well as in the previous chapters that the roots of literacy lie in the developing thought processes of the child. Skill is the handmaiden of, the liege to, meaning. Put in the obverse, form follows function. We cannot expect skill to emerge ahead of, or in isolation from, meaning. Instead, the search for meaning, stimulating the need for skill as it inevitably does, drives the organism to practice existing skills, forcing a process of branching and expansion of those skills, a creative activity in its own right, yet interdependent with and dependent upon meaning making or thinking, just as thinking, in association with experiencing, is the way in which new meanings, new thoughts, are created.

Growth in language power, whether the speaking-listening dyad or the writing-reading one, proceeds from an immature or incomplete state to maturity largely because the learner has opportunities to search for meaning through these avenues of knowing. That is not to say language in any of its forms comes into existence de novo, without arrangement or plan. Arrangements and plans take both indirect and direct forms, however. Children growing up in the United States find themselves in a language-rich environment, in a society bent on the goal of universal literacy. But we seem to have mistaken the differences in the roles of coaching and teaching, at least if in the latter instance we think of this activity as instructing rather than evoking, or educing, desired behaviors, the true meaning lying behind the word *education*.

As we have seen, particularly where speaking and writing are concerned, development follows a wavering but progressive course, full of errors, self-corrections, and forward leaps which are then subject to the same adjustments. As Piaget has told us (although we have not yet listened very well), error is not a "bad" thing; it is part of normal development. If children are not unnecessarily interfered with, they will use errors to promote their own growth toward fuller development. Not enough can be said about the importance and significance of what an educationist would call in shorthand, "an arranged environment." Whether it is at home or in the school, attention given to the quality of the environment should not be left to chance. The adult who plans an environment that is stimulating to the intellect and full of opportunities for playing (i.e., experimenting) with language in all its forms will be richly rewarded by evidences of language growth considerably beyond expectations.

Related Readings

Allen, R. V. (1976). *Language experiences in communication*. Boston, MA: Houghton Mifflin.

Applebee, A. N. (1978). *The child's concept of story — Ages two to seventeen.* Chicago: The University of Chicago Press.

Beach, R., & Bridewell, L. (Eds.). (1984). *New directions in composition research*. New York: Guilford Press.

Beers, J. W., & Henderson, E. H. (1977). A study of developing orthographic concepts among first graders. *Research in the Teaching of English, 11,* 133–148.

Buckley, M. H., & Boyle, O. (1981). *Mapping the writing journey*. Berkeley, CA: Bay Area Writing Project.

Burrows, A. T., et al. (1984). *They all want to write: Written English in the elementary school*. Hamden, CT: Library Professional Publications.

Calkins, L. M. (1983). *Lessons from a child: On the teaching and learning of writing*. Portsmouth, NH: Heinemann Educational Books.

Canney, G., & Schreiner, R. (1976–1977). A study of the effectiveness of selected syllabication rules and phonogram patterns for word attack. *Reading Research Quarterly, 12,* 102–124.

Chomsky, C. (1970). Reading, writing, and phonology. *Harvard Educational Review, 40,* 287–309.

Clark, M. M. (1975). *What did I write?* Auckland, NZ: Heinemann Educational Books.

Dyson, A. H. (1985). Puzzles, paints, and pencils: Writing emerges. *Educational Horizons, 64,* 13–16.

Elbow, P. (1973). *Writing without teachers.* New York: Oxford University Press.

Emig, J. (1983). *The web of meaning: Essays on writing, teaching, learning, and thinking.* Upper Montclair, NJ: Boynton Cook.

Esbensen, B. J. (1975). *A celebration of bees: Helping children write poetry.* New York: Winston Press.

Evanechko, P., et al. (1974). An investigation of the relationships between children's performance in written language and their reading ability. *Research in the Teaching of English, 8,* 315–326.

Graves, D. H. (1975). An examination of the writing processes of seven-year-old children. *Research in the Teaching of English, 9,* 227–241.

Graves, D. H. (1979). Let children show us how to help them write. *Visible Language, 13,* 16–28.

Hansen, J., et al. (1985). *Breaking ground: Teachers relate reading and writing in the elementary school.* Portsmouth, NH: Heinemann Educational Books.

Henderson, E. H., & Beers, J. W. (1980). *Developmental and cognitive aspects of learning to spell: A reflection of word knowledge.* Newark, DE: International Reading Association.

King, M. L., & Rentel, V. (1979). Toward a theory of early writing development. *Research in the Teaching of English, 13,* 255–264.

King, M. L., & Rentel, V. (1981). *How children learn to write: A longitudinal study.* Columbus, OH: Ohio University Research Foundation.

Lamme, L. L., & Childers, N. M. (1983). The composing processes of three young children. *Research in the Teaching of English, 17,* 31–50.

Nalven, F. B., & Augusto, J. (1972). How lasting are the effects of ITA vs. TO training in the development of children's creative writing? *Research in the Teaching of English, 6,* 17–19.

Newman, J. (1984). *The craft of children's writing.* New York: Scholastic Book Services.

Paul, R. (1976). Invented spelling in kindergarten. *Young Children, 31,* 195–200.

Read, C. (1975). Lessons to be learned from the preschool orthographer. In E. H. Lenneberg & E. Lenneberg (Eds.), *Foundations of language development* (vol. 2, pp. 329–346). New York: Academic Press.

Read, C. (1986). *Children's creative spelling.* New York: Routledge & Kegan Paul.

Rico, G. (1983). *Writing the natural way.* New York: Houghton Mifflin.

Schmandt-Besserat, D. (1978). The earliest precursor of writing. *Scientific American, 238,* 50–59.

Smith, F. (1982). *Writing and the writer.* New York: Holt, Rinehart & Winston.

Stewig, J. W. (1975). *Read to write: Using children's literature as a springboard to writing.* New York: Hawthorn Books.

Temple, C.A., et al. (1982). *The beginning of writing.* New York: Allyn & Bacon.

Walshe, R. D. (Ed.). (1982). *"Children want to write . . . ": Donald Graves in Australia.* Portsmouth, NH: Heinemann Educational Books.
Zutell, J. (1979). Spelling strategies of primary school children and their relationship to Piaget's concept of decentration. *Research in the Teaching of English, 13,* 69–80.

CHAPTER 8

Problems

Few families escape a sense of anxiety as their children approach school age, a feeling that intensifies as the time for them to actually go to school arrives. And for that ensuing period of a year or two, or even three, the time when we expect a youngster to establish his independence as a reader, not many parents can say they had few worries or concerns. At least that is the case in the United States, if only because so many youngsters in fact encounter difficulties of some kind.

It is to be expected that high levels of concern will be expressed where there is a high incidence of reading difficulties, and so it is not surprising that there have been many attempts to identify what might be called "causal factors," to identify the villain, so to speak. That search for the conditions that produce reading problems has been around a very long time. Beginning with the birth of the modern scientific era in the late 1800s, there have since been literally tens of thousands of studies designed to reveal the elusive nature of such difficulties. An interesting feature of inquiries into this troublesome subject is that virtually all of them have pursued topics implying that most reading problems are caused by some kind of internal malfunction that manifests itself in a processing failure, a breakdown in associating visual images with their appropriate auditory image. While the primary locus of difficulty is generally thought to be within the person, there is confusion over the precise reason for that failure to manifest itself. Some would have us believe the reason is organic, and a number of terms have been invented to describe that condition. Others, while conceding the existence of physiological barriers to the acquisition of print reading abilities, argue that a major source of difficulty lies in the way children are being taught. As I pointed out in an earlier chapter, for example, Jeanne Chall (1983a) has argued (and many have listened) that a "code-emphasis," or phonics, approach matches the way most children learn to read. Chall believes, incorrectly in my opinion, that adopting instructional practices that adhere to this view of how one learns to read would alleviate most of the problems.

While there is certainly reason to believe some reading problems are caused by an inner misfunctioning of one order or another, the very large number of reading problems can hardly be so easily explained. And when we compare that situation with what is found in such diverse societies as those we see in Scandinavia and Asia (I refer here particularly to Korea and Japan), where initial problems in the learning-to-read process are low, I believe it behooves us to be wary of any solution as simple, and as deceiving, as substituting one kind of stimulus set for another in an associationist bond. It would seem fairly obvious that these alternatives have been tried in various combinations for many years since Mann, and others, brought back the notion of whole-word and sentence methods. Repeated efforts to find a "best method" within the S-R bond have yielded no fruit worth eating. What we have before us in the fourth quarter of the twentieth century is little more than recrimination and criticism combined with a nostalgia for past practice.

In what follows, I discuss currently popular organic or physiologically based theories developed to explain why children have difficulty in the learning-to-read process. I then discuss other factors, such as the quality of home life, class grouping, and school tracking practices, that I believe are important in understanding the environment surrounding children as they attempt to learn to read but are infrequently cited as important to our understanding of the problem of reading. It is my contention these factors play a highly significant role in either facilitating or hampering youngsters in their reading development. Most if not all of them are potentially under the control of the school and open to modification.

Dyslexia Revisited

Who "Has" Dyslexia? Who Is Dyslexic?

"Dyslexia" is the oldest of the terms currently used to describe a problem in learning to read in which the reader is presumed to have the "intelligence" necessary but for some reason fails to perform as expected. There is now a widespread tendency among teachers, medical doctors, even parents, to declaim that someone, even themselves, "has" dyslexia, or is dyslexic. The presumption is that "dyslexia" exists as a diagnostic and prescriptive reality, that it describes a known physiological condition (or conditions), the consequence of which is a pronounced disability in reading print. Just the sound of the word lends a scientific aura to its use — and indeed, the term does derive from the medical literature, having been coined in the late 1800s when descriptions were reported in the medical literature of several individuals who were said to be suffering from "congenital word blindness." Although they were in the overall few in number, these cases represented a medical discovery of sorts, for it was the first recognition of the presence of a limited number of people in society who, not for lack of trying either on their own or their teacher's part, found great difficulty in learning to read. From these beginnings the term *dyslexia* was invented to describe the phenomenon in appropriately impressive terminology.

"Dyslexia," since it has neither diagnostic nor prescriptive power, at best tells us that someone believes a particular person ought to be able to read because there is presumed to be evidence of sufficient intelligence and there is no evidence of any of the anomalies commonly, although often· incorrectly, thought to be causal (usually visual or auditory defects). Given such meager information, it is little wonder the diagnosis provides no particular guide to what corrective measures will assist in remediating the condition. As such it is a useless, and often a condemning, term. In some circumstances it even becomes an excuse—for parents, teachers, and even the so-called "victims" themselves—to do nothing.

For all intents and purposes, then, we are substituting the term *dyslexia* for the old British one of "backwardness," providing us with nothing more than an identifying handle to describe someone who reads less well than intuition, with a little help from standardized tests, suggests to us he or she ought to.

Some New Terms for an Old Concept

Medical advances in recent years, particularly those in the field of neurobiology, have added greatly to our wealth of knowledge of how the brain seems to function. This development is at once fascinating, helpful, and yet misleading where the issue of reading development is concerned. On the one hand, there can be no question that new knowledge about many aspects of the brain has revolutionized many medical procedures. On the other, a real danger has developed that this new knowledge is leading us to make unwarranted assumptions and prescribe treatments that may be completely uncalled for.

Perhaps the most dangerous of these lies in the notion of "minimal brain dysfunction" and its corollary, the idea of "learning disabilities." We indeed now have instruments that measure various things within the realm of "brain function." But unless there is gross deviation from the normal (involving cases unseen in the usual school environment), we as yet do not have any directly useful links between particular abnormali ties and the presence of a problem in learning to read. Educationists have been quick to extrapolate on the idea of brain dysfunction, but since they know relatively little about neurobiology, they are, I believe, lacking in authority to speak to the subject. A little knowledge can in fact be a dangerous thing, but that has not put a damper on the tendency to attach one or another of these labels to youngsters, a tendency that has too often been aided and abetted by physicians who have little knowledge of reading behavior and language development. Like our other term, *minimal brain dysfunction* has a scientific ring to it; but also like it, the term itself is neither diagnostic nor prescriptive for a problem in learning to read.

The corollary term, *learning disabilities*, has also come into wide use in recent years. A recent estimate holds that 1.8 million children in American schools have been so diagnosed (Coles, 1987, p. 9), and many estimates run even higher. There has been little, if any, success in establishing a causal, neurologically based relationship with the development of fluent reading, a fact that seems to have affected neither the medical nor the teaching profession much, since so many continue to insist that important details of that relationship are known. Nor has it made much of an impression on many researchers who have discovered that, given the great public concern over "the reading problem," they can secure not only financial support but an overweening interest in what they have to say about the subject.

Various behavioral manifestations are said to accompany cases of learning disability. One of the most common is what is described as an "attention deficit." That is to say, children having difficulty with reading are perceived as being unable, for one reason or another, to focus their attention long enough to "learn." One outcome of this inability is reflected in the term *hyperactivity*. The hyperactive child is presumed to be one who is so driven to physical activity that he (or she, although it turns out almost all "hyperactive" children are males) is unable to give the necessary amount of attention to the instructional tasks that learning to read is said to require. Since the 1960s, an increasing number of physicians, as they have been attracted to a new subspecialty in medicine — treating children who are not performing up to expectations in school — have turned to chemical treatment programs. The drug of choice has been Ritalin, but there are others that produce similar results. For reasons not clearly understood, although Ritalin and similar drugs are classed as stimulants, on some children they apparently have quite an opposite, calming effect. "Hyperactivity" that responds to the administration of Ritalin and similar drugs presumably makes concentration on school work possible, something it is assumed would not otherwise happen. And of course concentration on the tasks involved in learning the subject matter of reading is what is important.

The question obviously arises as to whether hyperactivity is a true physiological condition requiring external controls of some sort. While it is clear that some children do manifest behaviors that interfere with their ability to perform successfully in a particular classroom, we still cannot be certain that the primary cause of that failure resides within the youngster. One factor that could stimulate such behavior is the extent to which the teacher develops a classroom environment so restrictive that hyperactive behavior inevitably occurs, at least on the part of one or two, or more, children. It is argued that more demands are currently being made on children's attention to tasks required of them, and that teachers themselves are more ready to label behavior disruptive; I believe this charge has some merit. Interestingly, "hyperactivity" is now being displaced in the lexicon of learning disorders with a new term, *attention deficit disorder* — A.D.D. is becoming a popular short form for the term. Whether or not this is more adequate as a descriptor, it demonstrates that hope is not being given up that the culprit in creating reading difficulties will yet be found residing within the individual.

It is understandable that we want to find causes of problems in learning to read. Labeling them lends a sense of security and suggests that the response required to correct the difficulty is at hand. In hyperactivity, and now attention deficit disorder, I believe we are in danger of labeling too many children with a term that may be appropriate for an extremely small subset of the number of children who are being so labeled. Certainly there are children who find the classroom and, though not as frequently, the home environment (and, indeed, the world in which they live) a difficult place to be. In my judgment, however, it behooves us to be very careful, and cautious, in concluding that the cause of these problems, and as a consequence the source of problems in learning to read, lies in some malfunction of the body's chemistry — and, furthermore, that it is appropriate to seek controls over behavior through medication with the expectation of improving reading as well as social behavior.

There is, unfortunately, a relatively new phenomenon that educationists are evidently beginning to face in growing numbers: Children born to mothers who use cocaine and other drugs often manifest behavioral disorders of various kinds. The extent to which learning problems stemming from maternal drug abuse can be ameliorated prior to entry into the formal educational setting remains to be seen. The effects, particularly of cocaine and others of the so-called hard drugs, have consequently provided medicine with yet another frontier. Given the evident wide use of such drugs throughout society, it appears likely no community will escape concern regarding the consequences stemming therefrom. And it remains unclear whether conventional treatments, such as the prescribing of Ritalin, will be appropriate for this new class of developmental problems.

Other Indicators of Sources of Difficulty in Learning to Read

Our friend E. B. Huey (1908), reflecting so long ago on the nature of reading behavior, was moved to write: "And so to completely analyze what we do when we read would almost be the acme of a psychologist's achievements, for it would be to describe very many of the most intricate workings of the human mind, as well as to unravel the tangled story of the most remarkable specific performance that civilization has learned in all its history" (p. 6). And so it would also be the "acme" of achievement to be able to predict the future occurrence of a problem in learning to read, for to know how the human animal learns to read would bring with it the power to understand why some children encounter problems in that regard. Yet the awesomeness of that task, while it did not escape Huey, surely has been missed by the many people who have tackled the question since, for the literature on the causes of reading problems and how they may be anticipated is a large one. And while the presence of a problem in learning to read print is usually all too evident — even though some individuals experiencing serious problems with reading manage to devise highly deceptive strategies allowing them to escape in large part the onus of such problems — our diagnostic and prescriptive tools remain in a rudimentary state. After all these years, more often than not the best we can do is hazard a guess as far as any individual case is concerned.

There are, however, some broad indicators that give us strong hints regarding why an individual is experiencing difficulty in developing an acceptable fluency in print reading. One that has been largely overlooked in the United States is family history. Several years ago, a study by Knud Herman (1959) in Denmark investigated the occurrence of reading problems in families. He traced medical and school histories through as many as four generations, discovering a recurrence through those generations, although not in any specific pattern. Sometimes a problem in learning to read print would appear in succeeding generations, more often than not on the male side, going from father to son (or uncle to nephew). Teachers in Scandinavia have commented to me about the frequency of occurrence within families. In a relatively stable society in which family history is a treasured part of everyday life and a "reading problem" is not something to be hidden, with the result that parents are much more likely to freely admit their own difficulties with learning to read, the role of family history as a major source of problems in learning to read can be seen more clearly. Further research in this area could contribute substantially to our understanding of the etiology of reading problems.

A second factor that very likely accounts for the appearance of reading problems in some children derives from exceptional medical histories. As we learn more about human variability, it becomes clear that the extent of the differences within human beings, and the concomitant differences that appear in exceptional cases, is extraordinarily wide. We do know that children experiencing problems in learning to read print generally present more instances of some kind of medical problem, usually several of them in some form of unique combination. Advances in neurobiology, particularly, increase our insights into how the human organism functions. Instrumentation is now at hand that reads the behavior of many aspects of the neural ganglia, the very activity of the neural pathways themselves. Even the thought process itself is being revealed in new dimensions. Print reading, for example, can be revealed as a neural process with such instrumentation. From these most recent of advances we will learn more about the inner workings of the mind. But much remains to be discovered, such as why a particular organism reacts in a certain way and, as importantly, what that may mean in the everyday world of school and learning.

The role of the eye and the ear in reading has been discussed in Chapter 4. However, it bears repeating that visual anomalies are rarely the cause of problems in learning to read. Severe problems may be disruptive to the process, but then, substitutes are available, and I refer here particularly to Braille. But the most common problem — the lack of adequate acuity for classroom tasks — while it well may make learning more uncomfortable, rarely interferes in any basic way. It is important for adults to be aware of the signs of such a problem: Inattentiveness, complaints of headaches and upset stomachs, and evidences of strain in any visual task at any distance are among the more common ones.

Auditory problems are another matter, of course. Persons who become profoundly deaf before speech is fairly firmly established, a stage usually reached around the age of 4, experience serious communicative disorders. The most significant of these is, as we might expect, the inability to hear the spoken language of others, and its obverse effect, the inability to speak normally, since speech must then, as Helen Keller pointed out, be acquired artificially. Lacking the ability to speak and to listen meaningfully has a devastating effect on the development of reading and writing abilities. An associated consequence is a disruption of cognitive or thought processes. Persons who have been profoundly deaf since birth or infancy rarely develop normal capabilities in either writing or reading.

Since the discovery of the sulfa drugs in the 1930s, and the subsequent development of other drugs of that class, the number of profoundly deaf children has decreased dramatically. Most causes of profound deafness now are heritable. However, a major health threat is still to be found in the disease of spinal meningitis, which can strike at any age, although its most vulnerable victims are in their earliest years. Untreated, or improperly treated because of a misdiagnosis, spinal meningitis, if survived, produces deafness, usually of a profound nature. While the most tragic instances of meningitis are those children who were stricken before an oral language had developed to the point where tonality and syntax were thoroughly established, the sudden onset of profound deafness from spinal meningitis has tragic consequences surrounding it for any age. The inability to participate freely in oral conversation with another inevitably leads to an isolation few hearing people can understand.

Of growing concern is the question of the possible effect other diseases may have on hearing, particularly here as it relates to language development. A very common disorder among children is infections of the middle ear, a condition referred to in the medical world as *otitis media*. Little is as yet known whether there is a direct linkage between such infections and the reading/writing dyad, or perhaps upon language development generally. However, particularly where otitis media becomes chronic, as is too often the case, we do know we have a situation in which hearing is impaired. Since we understand something of the significance of the relationship of hearing to language development, it behooves us to give our close attention to any child who is so afflicted. Medical research is moving very rapidly in developing an understanding of this disease, and we may therefore hope to see a lessening of its presence in the school population.

The Significance of Home and Family Life

It would simplify matters immeasurably if we could be assured that problems in learning to read were found to be the result of such things as "dyslexia" or "minimal brain dysfunction," or were in some other fashion primarily due to some kind of organic problem; or that such problems were caused by an inappropriate method of instruction. What a relief it would be if we could establish that English is such an irregularly perverse language that learning to deal with it in its printed form precludes the possibility of near universal success in mastering it.

The situation is otherwise, of course, and so we need to turn our attention to those things operative in a youngster's life that have the potential for promoting the kind of cognitive confusion I have referred to earlier, or that might be helpful in securing success in the learning-to-read process.

From all that has come before, the reader will surely realize how singularly important I believe the home environment is at every age, but especially during those earliest years through the age when independence in reading print is well established. Surely no other time can be as important in the overall development of any youngster.

Awareness of the importance of the preschool years in assuring a successful start, and continued achievement, has been with us for a very long time. E. B. Huey (1908) commented on its significance when he wrote,

> The secret of it all lies in parents' reading aloud to and with the child. . . . All that is needed is books of good old jingles and rhymes and folk stories and fairy tales, with illustrative pictures, and a mother or father or friend who cares enough for the children to . . . read aloud to them. The child will keep it up by the hour and the week and the month, and his natural learning to read is only a question of time. (pp. 332–333)

Because parents still hold the power to construct, either by deliberate intent or by default, the basic kind of environment in which their youngsters will be nourished, what Huey had to say is as relevant today as it was in 1900. Unhappily, the reality is that more often than not the home environment is likely to emerge in topsy-turvy fashion rather than by careful design. Huey recognized this likelihood and recommended that the early years of school replicate the ideal home in as many ways as possible. If children did not gain independence in reading in that environment, he would then institute more formal instruction, around the age of 10.

Such notions about what the home environment should be like stir little controversy, until the school is part of the scenery. Not surprisingly, it has been popular to scoff at suggestions that formal instruction be delayed. And while there have always been those who have argued that the learning-to-read process is best supported by the kind of school environment Huey, and others like him since, had in mind, traditional notions that reading should be taught for its own sake have persisted (Moore & Moore, 1977). The reader of these pages will have to make a personal judgment regarding which position appears more warranted. Certainly, one could not disagree that the American family needs a great deal of strengthening, and few would disagree that children should begin their lives in an atmosphere rich in books and presided over by parents who do just as Huey suggests.

Reading and School Life

The Early Years

As I have shown, almost every child entering school is able to read many common labels and logos, and a surprisingly large number also find old friends in print even when those familiar words are not imbedded contextually. This number includes the child coming from a meager home environment who, nonetheless, surrounded by words, has entered the world of print language, whether consciously or not. And of course, many, probably most, are not aware that they can in fact read print. The majority of 5- and 6-year-olds believe that "reading," whatever that might be, is learned in the first grade and is unrelated to life out of school.

Unhappily, most teachers seem to share this view. Like the linguist who will admit the existence of language only after single words are joined together into meaningful patterns, there is a reluctance to think of children reading print unless it is arranged in what purports to be a meaningful sequence, preferably in a book. The consequence is a classroom climate that rejects out-of-school or "worldly" achievements where print is concerned, and that focuses on reading for its own sake, as an end in itself. It is therefore not surprising to find that the overwhelming majority of teachers utilize a methodology intended to *invoke* the ability to read print, to teach reading as a subject in the school curriculum. Thus the major accoutrement of the reading "lesson" is the textbook, supplemented with a number of materials, some directly connected to individual lessons in the text, others less so.

From the first day of school on, children are sorted through a process that seeks to identify the level of "readiness" each is perceived to have attained for dealing successfully with the formal instruction in reading that is to come no later than the first grade. Over the years a number of tests assessing reading readiness (see Chapter 6 for a discussion of readiness itself) have been devised to facilitate the sorting process. Concepts about what children need to know to become more "ready" for print reading—to succeed in the world of textbooks, workbooks, and achievement tests—have been turned into ideas for teaching children to do things it is assumed will prepare them for "real" reading beginning no later than the first grade. "Pre-reading" materials place heavy emphasis upon exercises that employ symbols of various kinds (although not words themselves) and require the child to manipulate those symbols in what, for want of a better term, might be called a reading-like activity. All of the problems of learning to read print are thought to be included in these exercises, but without the use of words themselves. Instead, representations are employed, some as realistic as line drawings will allow, others more abstract in nature.

My concern here is not with a detailed criticism of the value of these exercises, however, despite their many problems, but with the sorting process itself. For with these first attempts to segregate children into layers of "readiness," and to provide instruction assumed to be appropriate (and, we would hope, meaningful), we find the beginnings of what I consider to be an insidious system that has all the odious qualities of real-world segregation policies. As children are moved through the graded school system, they are separated into groups selected on the basis of how well each child seems to deal with the lessons contained in the particular textbook series. What we discover on closer examination is that, for most children, the formation of these achievement/ability groups in kindergarten and first grade results in a permanent within-class assignment that lasts beyond the elementary school years; it continues in junior and senior high school, and its effects linger on into post-secondary forms of education and into life after school as well.

Everyone is aware of the kind of status that reading group membership assigns. Whether there are many teachers who give names to their three groups as the one who, the story goes, called them her "Bluebirds," "Yellowbirds," and "Crows," the truth of the comparison comes through to those who suffer membership, particularly for those who are "Crows," in many ways over many years of school. For although the children are unaware of it, these are in effect permanent assignments: Few children will join another reading group during their elementary school experience, and when a change does come, the chances are the movement will be downward, to a "lower" reading group.

If ability grouping were a demonstrably superior way of organizing children for instruction in reading, we might well be justified in teaching within the classroom structure it dictates. And there is certainly no dearth of research, for this area of concern has gained the avid attention of researchers since the 1920s. However, much of it is seriously flawed for several reasons. Perhaps the most significant reason lies in the very concept of homogeneousness itself. In considering the possibility of identifying children with closely similar if not identical abilities or achievement, we place ourselves at the mercy of two difficult problems. The lesser of these is the problem the tests themselves pose. I have already suggested some of the difficulties we encounter in even assessing reading ability. At their very best, tests report to us only the residue of actual reading, information based on the recall of what has been read. Additionally, they give us information about how much a child knows of what we perceive the mechanics of reading to be, the kinds of information a child has about the reading act itself: knowledge of phonics, grammatical rules, and so forth. This kind of information is hardly a complete report of either reading ability or achievement.

The other, more important dimension lies in the nature of human variability. If we were able to get an accurate fix on either ability or achievement, we would discover that even within a small group — the size of a typical class — human variation is so great it is not possible to form a truly "homogeneous" group on any measure. When reading groups are formed on the basis of achievement on a test score, or on any other measure, therefore, only the range of variation is reduced. And of course the degree to which this can be accomplished is entirely dependent upon the initial characteristics of the group (see, for example, Goodlad & Anderson, 1987).

Early on in the child's school experience, then, we see a system that assigns each boy and girl to an instructional group that carries with it either the sweet smell of success or the sour one of failure. Because, for inexplicable reasons, more boys experience difficulty in the learning-to-read process (at least in the United States), membership in these groups is badly skewed. Girls predominate in the "high" group, boys in the "low." From the beginning, each youngster is assigned a status, an implied sense of worth, one that, because of the relative permanence of the groupings thus formed, will be reinforced as the years go by.

The Middle Years

Schools in the United States are structured around different patterns. By far the most common is referred to in the shorthand as a 6-3-3 system. Here there is an elementary school of 6 years (there may or may not be a kindergarten), a "junior high" of 3 years, and a 3-year high school. The more traditional 8-4 school is now found in some, usually rural, areas where the population growth has not required extensive new building. Recently, the idea of a "middle-school" has attracted approving attention as an alternative to the junior high school, an institution increasingly seen as having failed in its mission as a transitional institution for the abominable adolescent years. Such schools follow either a 5-4-3, 6-2-4, or, more rarely, 4-4-4 plan. Within these varying organizational patterns, textbook publishers provide "basal" readers, that coordinated set of instructional materials designed to provide the teacher with everything needed to teach children to read through the first eight years. As I have noted, there is almost universal use of one or another of these "basal reader series" through the first six years, at least. The amount of direct instruction in reading required in the seventh and eighth year will depend largely on the success a child has in the previous six years of formal instruction.

When the time arrives for a youngster to go on to the second tier school, usually the junior high school, the student will in most instances go to a much larger school. This is because several elementary schools usually feed into one junior high or middle school. The youngster has now come to the end of a school experience in what is called a "self-contained" classroom, one in which one teacher has taught all the "subjects" and reading instruction has been premised upon achievement/ ability grouping. Still harboring the notion that teaching, if not learning as well, is eased (at least for those with sufficient seniority to commandeer classrooms populated by able readers) when students are grouped according to their ability to read print, the obvious way to assign students to their classes is to "track" them. It is at this point that reading ability becomes the critical factor in school success. Assigning youngsters according to their past record as readers, earned through the elementary school years, the junior high or middle school commonly and deliberately establishes a hierarchy of strands or tracks in which ability and achievement become increasingly fused.

At this level we begin to see clearly the major consequence of the emphasis of form over function that has dominated instruction in the elementary school. Now we have before us a very obvious and large number of youngsters who cannot "read for meaning," as the cliché goes. Recall the saying, "First one learns to read, and then one reads to learn." The evidence suggests that, no matter what test scores they achieve in the elementary years, as books become more central as sources for information and as mastery of their content increasingly becomes the criterion for school success, a very large part of the junior high school student population is in deep trouble.

One doesn't need to go very far to understand why a youngster may give indications of successful learning in the elementary school (through test scores, the ability to complete various exercises, and other indications of skill development) and yet run into difficulty later on. Instruction that gives such short shrift to meaning — to what print reading is all about — is bound to be vacuous. Without the substance of meaning, skill learning becomes not only meaningless, but useless, and unavailable when needed.

If there is one thing that youngsters experiencing difficulty at this level have in common, it is the failure to understand the meaning of reading. They are locked into the notion that reading requires, first above all else, quite literally, the ability to "say" each word in order, and they are absolutely stumped when a word is encountered that they cannot say aloud. The idea that reading generates meanings is foreign to them; the possibility that meaning is available even if one skips a word is beyond their comprehension.

Beyond Adolescence

Patterns of grouping typical of the middle school become institutionalized in the senior high school. Students tracked into achievement classes that originated in the elementary classroom reading group are now further refined into general courses of study. Successful readers gravitate toward the academic curriculum, while the others find themselves in what is sometimes called a general curriculum, or else in a Voc-Ed (vocational education) course of study. Still others, having found their way into trouble in and out of school, either drop out or enroll in an alternative high school program. Except in the academic curriculum, the problem of inadequate reading ability persists. For many of these students, instruction in reading continues, either as a concern of subject-area teachers or, as is often the case, in settings designed to work on reading skills directly.

It is unnecessary to dwell here in any detail on the social, economic, and personal consequences that result from the failure to educate so large a segment of the population. Employers, the police, and legislators face them directly every day, but all of us are affected in one way or another. This problem constitutes a clear and present danger to every segment of society.

But let us take the story just a bit further, into our colleges and universities. Adult reading is now a concern throughout most of higher education. Community colleges as well as four-year institutions have over the past twenty years discovered the necessity of offering courses designed to help students whose reading, and consequently study habits, is retarding their ability to function successfully in these institutions.

In Sum

All children come to school with a common expectation, that they will learn to read. At that point in their young lives, their world is a relatively small one, encompassing the home, the school, and the immediate neighborhood, but with glimmerings of other worlds brought to them primarily through television and the cinema. That world expands as the years go by, not so much in its physical dimensions as in the quality and kind of human relationships making their appearance in that environment. Youngsters who do not succeed in school begin, I believe, to find greater attractions in the out-of-school world simply because it is a place where they can escape memories of the troubles they are experiencing in the classroom. No one needs reminding that there are some environments that invite asocial behavior, no matter what. But my point is simply this: School failure, which is universally defined by the inability to develop fluent reading, exacerbates an already difficult situation with each year. Youngsters in trouble with reading gravitate to others in the same boat, giving rise to a vicious cycle that is difficult, if not impossible, to break.

Adding to the difficulty is the public's apparent inability or even unwillingness to make decisive efforts to deal with the problem of a youth population without skills and, essentially, without hope. The history of American public education is one of heaping responsibility for various social ills on the schools. School people have, for their part, been naive in believing they could be effective in dealing with such diverse problems as teenage pregnancies, gang activity, alcohol and drug abuse — the list is long indeed. It is not unreasonable to suggest that the arrival of so many problems at the schoolhouse door has long diverted attention away from more central goals of the nation's schools.

So serious is the problem that some are giving up hope our schools can continue to cope. For example, John Holt wrote several widely read books during the 1960s and 1970s, *How Children Fail* and *How Children Learn* among them, that were basically constructive in tone. Later, having given up on the possibility of change, Holt became a leader of a movement that encouraged parents to keep their children out of school, to educate them at home. Jonathan Kozol, in his book *Illiterate America*, suggests that the problem of illiteracy should be attacked through adult education programs, but not programs run by the schools. At the least, he fails to articulate a role for the public school system in solving the reading problem.

Certainly, there is reason for pessimism. The schools seem to be paralyzed as they try to solve the problem of reading by perseverating conventional instructional practices. The teaching of reading in that formal sense now occupies a very large portion of the school day in our elementary schools. It has become a certainty that children who fail to become fluent readers during these formative years can expect to continue to study reading into the middle or junior high school. Of those who stay in school beyond that point, many will need remedial help in high school, and even in college.

Related Readings

Allington, R. L. (1980). Poor readers don't get to read much in reading groups. *Language Arts, 57,* 872–877.

Beckerman, T. M., & Good, T. L. (1981). The classroom ratio of high and low aptitude students and its effect on achievement. *American Educational Research Journal, 18,* 317–327.

Cogan, J. J. (1975). Elementary teachers as nonreaders. *Phi Delta Kappan, 56,* 495–496.

Critchley, M. (1978). *Dyslexia defined.* Springfield, IL: Charles C. Thomas.

Eder, D. (1981). Ability grouping as a self-fulfilling prophecy: A micro-analysis of teacher-student interaction. *Sociology of Education, 54,* 151–162.

Esposito, D. (1973). Homogeneous and heterogeneous ability grouping: Principal findings and implications for evaluating and designing more effective environments. *Review of Educational Research, 43,* 163–179.

Franklin, B. (1987). *Learning disability: Dissenting essays.* Philadelphia: Falmer Press.

Glasser, W. (1984). *Control theory: A new explanation of how we control our lives.* New York: Harper & Row.

Glasser, W. (1986). *Control theory in the classroom.* New York: Harper & Row.

Halgren, B. (1950). *Specific dyslexia: A clinical and genetic study.* Stockholm.

Haller, E. J., & Davis, S. A. (1980). Does socioeconomic status bias the assignment of elementary school students to reading groups? *American Educational Research Journal, 17,* 409–418.

Haller, E. J., & Davis, S. A. (1981). Teacher perceptions, parental social status, and grouping for reading instruction. *Sociology of Education, 54,* 162–174.

Haskins, R., et al. (1983). Teacher and student behavior in high- and low-ability groups. *Journal of Educational Psychology, 75,* 865–876.

Johnston, P. H. (1985). Understanding reading disability: A case study approach. *Harvard Educational Review, 55,* 153–177.

Monroe, M. (1932). *Children who cannot read.* Chicago: University of Chicago Press.

Morgenstern, A. (Ed.). (1966). *Grouping in the elementary school.* New York: Pitman.

Mour, S. I. (1977). Do teachers read? *The Reading Teacher, 30,* 397–401.

Rosenholtz, S. J., & Simpson, C. (1984). The formation of ability conceptions: Developmental trend or social construction. *Review of Educational Research, 54,* 31–63.

Rowan, B., & Miracle, A. W. (1983). Systems of ability grouping and the stratification of achievement in elementary schools. *Sociology of Education, 56,* 133–144.

Sigmon, S. B. (1987). *Radical analysis of special education: Focus on historical development and learning disabilities.* Philadelphia: Falmer Press.

Strike, K. A. (1983). Fairness and ability grouping. *Educational Theory, 33,* 3–4.

Valtin, R. (1979). Dyslexia: Deficit in reading or deficit in research? *Reading Research Quarterly, 14,* 201–221.

Veldman, D. J., & Sanford, J. P. (1984). The influence of class ability level on student achievement and classroom behavior. *American Educational Research Journal, 21,* 629–644.

Vellutino, F. R. (1977). Alternative conceptualizations of dyslexia: Evidence in support of a verbal-deficit hypothesis. *Harvard Educational Review, 47,* 334–354.

Weinstein, R. S. (1976). Reading group membership in first grade: Teacher behavior and pupil experience over time. *Journal of Educational Psychology, 68,* 103–116.

Afterword

On these pages I have attempted to develop a rationale for thinking differently about the problem of reading that may be of help to the reader who is looking for an alternative perspective on the problem of literacy. I have tried to illuminate the essence of traditional thinking about the reading process and how one learns to read with fluency, contrasting it with quite a different view that is both old and new. Beginning in the latter part of the nineteenth century, when reading as a process first began to be studied seriously, there have been psychologists, philosophers, and educationists who have turned a wary eye on the idea that the learning-to-read process is but a simple matter of engaging the most efficient instructional techniques. They have thought of it as a manifestation of a complex orchestration of physiological factors — the visual and auditory, the tactile and kinaesthetic, the neuro-muscular system generally — with thought processes, which are themselves the consequence of the intellect interacting in a social milieu.

Reading was seen as a mystery, and they concluded that, if a child were to acquire this ability, it probably would best occur outside the bounds of traditional ways of teaching. They assumed, I think correctly, that the vehicle for development would be practice, and that the fuel which would make practice happen would be the quest for meaning. They believed that purpose directed behavior and that the quest for meaning drove the organism to practice, which, in its turn, provided the basis for growth and development.

In this sense, the idea is a relatively old one. It dates from the very period that gave rise to schools as we know them today. But that view of the problem of reading was a naive one because so little was known about child language. It was also an idea that fell outside of the main-stream of psychological thought. The history of ideas documents the extraordinary influence theories of associationism, from which grew today's behaviorally based psychology, have had on teaching practice. In the face of such an overwhelming acceptance of a psychology of learning, it is perhaps surprising to find that the naturalistic view has survived through the years since. In another sense, however, it is not so surprising, for the intellectual roots of psychology are in philosophy. Today, as then, our philosophical biases unsuspectingly color many aspects of our lives, among them what we believe about what makes human beings tick, including how we think they learn, and in this case, specifically, how we think they learn to read.

Learning to read by reading is new in that the rationale in support of this approach to the problem of literacy is now increasingly finding its base in research rather than in a philosophy of life. I have tried to show that studies of oral language development provide a solid base for understanding that acquiring verbal language, in all its forms (oral, aural, reading print, and writing) is not the mechanistic process behavioral psychologists have led us to believe. Instead, it is a constructive process directed almost entirely from within, brought into flower through an inner desire to know and to communicate, to be in verbal touch with others. While we have yet much to learn about language development, and while the how of language acquisition remains almost as much a mystery today as it was a hundred years ago, knowledge acquired over the last quarter century at the least provides a sound basis for a rationale to guide conducting "instruction" in print reading and writing other than the one that has dominated in our schools and classrooms, with such disastrous results.

If that rationale is as soundly based as I believe it to be, who will listen, and who will act upon it? No one should be so naive as to think that the conventional wisdom is ever easily upset, particularly where schools are concerned. They are institutions bound by tradition. Change comes slowly, if at all. To set upon the problem of securing change in any educational setting will be frustrating and unrewarding. If change is to come, it will be the result of individuals changing. That kind of change starts at home, within the person who wishes to do things differently.

I have in these pages approached the question of methodology obliquely, if at all. There is no "one way" to do anything, nor is there a "my way" others should emulate, if not copy, textbook declarations to the contrary notwithstanding. And, whenever a teacher or parent sets out to modify his or her way of behaving with children, movement away from the old toward something new or different necessarily is a difficult and gradual process, not one in which the old is here today but gone tomorrow. All teaching is, or should be, driven by attempts to find a greater harmony between goals and method. There is consequently always a dynamic tension between what we do and what we want to achieve in teaching as well as in parenting. Someone else's method can therefore only be suggestive, but it can also be helpful. There are many writers who address the question of method structured to enhance an experiential approach to language development. Some of these I have listed in the Related Readings found at the end of each chapter and in the References.

Today's schools are in many ways caught between a rock and a hard place, a condition that is preventing experimentation and change just when it is most needed. On the one hand, the American public is angry and frustrated over the seeming inability of the schools to solve the problem of literacy, now endemic in this country. On the other, and in reaction to the hostility being expressed in legislatures and other public bodies and throughout the private sector, school people, not surprisingly, are responding with increased rigidity. Teachers inevitably lose autonomy in that kind of climate. The consequence is education by fiat. Principals and others in the central administration are increasingly involving themselves in decision making that effectively controls the parameters in which teachers may make decisions about what will happen in the classroom. One way this is done is through selection of instructional materials. Decisions are now often made without reference to the preference of the teaching staff, and the results of this practice strongly imply that reading instruction will be in accordance with a particular textbook series. Another avenue for this kind of coercion is found in the kind of in-service activity the administration arranges for teachers. No longer is it unusual for administrative staff to employ consultants whose in-service programs are designed to implement a particular instructional pattern throughout a school district. Most obvious, perhaps, are the attempts to control teacher behavior directly through supervision and evaluation techniques, a not-so-subtle means of obtaining conforming behavior.

It is ironic that the American educational enterprise is uniquely equipped to foster this situation. In bringing the "whole-word" method across the Atlantic, Horace Mann also brought the organizational structure we see today in our elementary schools, essential elements of which have been extended into the secondary school. It is a framework based on authoritarian principles, selected for its apparent efficiency, but installed in an institution designed to foster democratic principles. After adding on several higher levels of management, we see now an institution whose efforts to change and improve rely on utilizing what has been called a "trickle-down" or "top-down" theory of curriculum development. The contrasting view of how curriculum changes can occur is the "bottom-up" or "grass roots" approach. "Top-down" strategies tend to reinforce the status quo because there is usually a vested interest in demonstrating that the organization is already successful in what it is doing, that "change" implies improving within an existing frame. It is in this climate that the teaching of reading generally tends to take place.

But there is still a place for the person who would march to a different drummer, as long as the rhythm of that beat is not sounded too loudly. Doing so is not easy in a profession rooted in loneliness. Because professional interaction is not usually part of the teaching act itself — teachers work "alone" as professionals even when they are in the classroom — it is not surprising to find what often appears to be an inordinate need to inform and proselytize. Teachers tend to be zealots, I am afraid, and that tendency causes a lot of trouble. But possibilities exist for teachers who hanker to break away from the crowd, since their essential aloneness makes it difficult for others to tell what they are doing. Thomas Jefferson once advocated, in a letter to a friend, "a little revolution now and then," remarking that a democracy could not grow, or even survive, if coercive forces threatened to prevent its proper development, and that resistance to such forces was in fact appropriate in a democratic society. That principle may well apply when we think of the coercive circumstances preventing teachers from teaching in the best way they know how.

REFERENCES

INDEX

ABOUT THE AUTHOR

References

Allen, R. V. (1961). The language-experience approach to reading. In M. P. Douglass (Ed.). *Claremont Reading Conference, 25th yearbook* (pp. 59–66). Claremont, CA: The Claremont Graduate School.

Armantage, A. A. (1986). *Reassessing the implications of Piaget's theory for reading instruction: A comparison of the cognitive and art development of early readers of print and their yet-to-read peers.* Unpublished doctoral dissertation, the Claremont Graduate School, Claremont, CA.

Beers, J. W., et al. (1977). The logic behind children's spelling. *Elementary School Journal, 77,* 238–242.

Bissex, G. L. (1973). *Gnys at wrk: A child learns to write and read.* Cambridge, MA: Harvard University Press.

Bond, G. L., & Dykstra, R. (1967). The cooperative research program in first-grade reading. *Reading Research Quarterly, 3* (entire issue).

Bormuth, J. R. (1973–1974). Reading literacy: Its definition and assessment. *Reading Research Quarterly, 9,* 7–66.

Bryant, P., & Bradley, L. (1985). *Children's reading problems: Psychology and education.* Oxford: Basil Blackwell.

Burmeister, L. (1968). Usefulness of phonic generalizations. *The Reading Teacher, 21,* 349–356.

Chall, J. S. (1983a). *Learning to read: The great debate* (rev. ed.). New York: McGraw-Hill. (Original work published 1967)

Chall, J. S. (1983b). *Stages of reading development.* New York: McGraw-Hill.

Chomsky, C. (1971). Write first, read later. *Childhood Education, 47,* 296–299.

Chomsky, N. (1970). Phonology and reading. In H. Levin & J. P. Williams (Eds.), *Basic studies on reading* (pp. 3–18). New York: Basic Books.

Chukovsky, K. (1968). *From two to five* (M. Morton, Trans.). Berkeley, CA: University of California Press.

Clifford, G. J. (1984). *Buch und lesen:* Historical perspectives on literacy and schooling. *Review of Educational Research, 54,* 472–500.

Clymer, T. (1963). The utility of phonic generalizations in the primary grades. *The Reading Teacher, 16,* 252–258.

Coles, G. (1987). *The learning mystique: A critical look at "learning disabilities."* New York: Pantheon Books.

Coser, L., et al. (1982). *Books: The culture and commerce of publishing.* New York: Basic Books.

Curti, M. (1959). *The social ideas of American educators.* Patterson, NJ: Little-field, Adams.

Curtiss, S. (1977). *Genie: A linguistic study of a modern-day "wild child."* New York: Academic Press.

Dallman, M., et al. (1982). *The teaching of reading* (6th ed.). New York: Holt, Rinehart & Winston. (Original work published 1960)

Davis, R. H. (1984). Auditory evoked potentials. In R. H. Nodar & C. Barber (Eds.), *Evoked potentials II: The second international evoked potentials symposium.* London: Butterworth.

Delacato, C. (1963). *The diagnosis and treatment of reading problems.* Spring-field, IL: Charles C. Thomas.

Dewey, J. (1938). *Experience and education.* New York: Macmillan.

Doman, G. J. (1965). *Teach your baby to read.* London: Cape.

Douglass, M. P. (1969). Beginning reading in Norway. *The Reading Teacher, 23,* 17-22+.

Downing, J. (1968). The implications of research on children's thinking for the early stages of reading. In M. P. Douglass (Ed.), *Claremont Reading Conference, 32nd yearbook* (pp. 206-213). Claremont, CA: The Claremont Graduate School.

Downing, J. (1969). How children think about reading. *The Reading Teacher, 3,* 217-230.

Downing, J. (1970). The development of linguistic concepts in children's think-ing. *Research in the Teaching of English, 4,* 5-19.

Downing, J. (1971-1972). Children's developing concepts of spoken and written language. *Journal of Reading Behavior, 4,* 1-19.

Downing, J. (1973-1974). The child's conception of a "word." *Reading Research Quarterly, 9,* 568-582.

DuCharme, C. C. (1987). Children as readers and writers in the classroom: An impossible dream? In M. P. Douglass (Ed.), *Claremont Reading Conference, 51st yearbook* (pp. 165-176). Claremont, CA: The Claremont Grad-uate School.

Durkin, D. (1966). *Children who read early: Two longitudinal studies.* New York: Teachers College Press.

Durkin, D. (1974-1975). A six year study of children who learned to read in school at the age of four. *Reading Research Quarterly, 10,* 9-61.

Durkin, D. (1978-1979). What classroom observations reveal about reading comprehension instruction. *Reading Research Quarterly, 14,* 481-533.

Edwards, B. (1979). *Drawing on the right side of the brain: A course in enhanc-ing creativity and artistic confidence.* Los Angeles: J. P. Tarcher.

Emans, R. (1967). The usefulness of phonics generalizations above the primary grades. *The Reading Teacher, 20,* 419-425.

Fernald, G. M. (1943). *Remedial techniques in basic school subjects.* New York: McGraw-Hill.

Fromkin, V., et al. (1985). The development of language in Genie: A case of language acquisition beyond the "critical period." In V. Clark et al. (Eds.), *Language* (4th ed.). New York: St. Martin's Press.

Furth, H.G. (1966). *Thinking without language: Psychological implications of deafness.* New York: The Free Press.

Furth, H.G. (1974). Reading as thinking: A developmental perspective. In F. B. Murray & J. J. Pikulski (Eds.), *The acquisition of reading: Cognitive, linguistic and perceptual prerequisites* (pp. 43–54). Baltimore: University Park Press.

Furth, H. G. (1986). *Piaget for teachers* (2nd ed.). Washington, DC: Author. (Original work published 1970)

Gardner, H. (1978, March–April). What we know (and don't know) about the two halves of the brain. *Harvard Magazine*, pp. 24–27.

Gates, A. I. (1937). The necessary mental age for beginning reading. *Elementary School Journal, 37*, 497–508.

Ginsburg, H., & Opper, S. (1979). *Piaget's theory of intellectual development* (2d ed.). Englewood Cliffs, NJ: Prentice-Hall.

Goodlad, J. I. (1984). *A place called school.* New York: McGraw-Hill.

Goodlad, J. I., & Anderson, R. H. (1987). *The nongraded elementary school* (2d Ed.). New York: Teachers College Press.

Goodman, K. S. (1969). Analysis of oral reading miscues: Applied linguistics. *Reading Research Quarterly, 5*, 9–30.

Goodman, K. S. (1976a). Behind the eye: What happens in reading. In H. Singer & R. B. Ruddell (Eds.), *Theoretical models and processes of reading* (2nd ed.) (pp. 470–497). Newark, DE: International Reading Association.

Goodman, K. S. (1976b). Reading: A psycholinguistic guessing game. In H. Singer & R. B. Ruddell (Eds.), *Theoretical models and processes of reading* (2nd ed.) (pp. 497–508). Newark, DE: International Reading Association.

Goodman, Y. M. (1980). The roots of literacy. In M. P. Douglass (Ed.), *Claremont Reading Conference, 44th yearbook* (pp. 1–32). Claremont, CA: The Claremont Graduate School.

Goodman, Y. M. (1984). The development of initial literacy. In A. O. Goelman & F. Smith (Eds.), *Awakening to Literacy* (pp. 102–109). Portsmouth, NH: Heinemann Educational Books.

Gould, S. J. (1981). *The mismeasure of man.* New York: Norton.

Gray, W. S. (1960). *On their own in reading: How to give children independence in analyzing new words* (rev. ed.). Chicago: Scott, Foresman. (Original work published 1948)

Haley, A. (1976). *Roots.* New York: Doubleday.

Hanna, P. R., et al. (1966). *Phoneme-grapheme correspondences as cues to spelling improvement.* Washington, DC: Government Printing Office, U.S. Office of Education.

Hartzog, C. P. (1984). Notebooks and PCs: A writing curriculum for the '80s. In M. P. Douglass (Ed.), *Claremont Reading Conference, 48th yearbook* (pp. 81–86). Claremont, CA: The Claremont Graduate School.

Henderson, E. (1985). *Teaching spelling.* New York: Houghton Mifflin.

Henderson, E. H., Estes, T., & Stonecash, S. (1972). An exploratory study of word acquisition among first graders at mid-term in language experience approach. *Journal of Reading Behavior, 4,* 21–30.

Hermann, K. (1959). *Reading disability: A medical study of word-blindness and related handicaps.* Springfield IL: Charles C. Thomas.

Hockett, J. C. (1938). *The vocabularies and contents of elementary school readers.* State of California, Department of Education Bulletin, No. 3.

Hodges, R. E. (1981). *Learning to spell.* Urbana, IL: ERIC Clearing House on Reading and Communication Skills and the National Council of Teachers of English.

Hodges, R. E. (1982). *Improving spelling and vocabulary in the secondary school.* Urbana, IL: ERIC Clearing House on Reading and Communication Skills and the National Council of Teachers of English.

Hodges, R. E. (1983). The concept of structure and learning to spell. In M. P. Douglass (Ed.). *Claremont Reading Conference, 47th yearbook* (pp. 37–43). Claremont, CA: The Claremont Graduate School.

Hodges, R. E., & Rudorf, E. H. (Eds.). (1972). *Language and learning to read: What teachers should know about language.* New York: Houghton Mifflin.

Holt, J. C. (1964). *How children fail.* New York: Pitman.

Holt, J. C. (1967). *How children learn.* New York: Pitman.

Hopper, R., & Naremore, R. C. (1973). *Children's speech: A practical introduction to communication development.* New York: Harper & Row.

Huey, E. B. (1908). *The psychology and pedagogy of reading.* New York: Macmillan; rpt., Cambridge, MA: M.I.T. Press, 1968.

Hunter, M. (1976). Right-brained kids in left-brained schools. *Today's Education, 65,* 45–48.

Jenkins, L. (1978). *The relationships between cognitive development, language development, and reading ability in children ages six to nine.* Unpublished Doctoral Dissertation, The Claremont Graduate School, Claremont, CA.

Johns, J. (1972). Children's concepts of reading and their reading achievements. *Journal of Reading Behavior, 4,* 56–57.

Joos, M. (1964). Language and the school child. *Harvard Educational Review, 34,* 203–210.

Kennedy, H. (1963). Problems in aural reading. In M. P. Douglass (Ed.), *Claremont Reading Conference, 27th yearbook* (pp. 86–100). Claremont, CA: The Claremont Graduate School.

Kolls, M. (1980). *A study of relationships between cognitive development, drawing development and spontaneous speech among children ages five through eight.* Unpublished doctoral dissertation, The Claremont Graduate School, Claremont, CA.

Kozol, J. (1985). *Illiterate America.* New York: Anchor Press/Doubleday.

LaBerge, D., & Samuels, S. J. (1985). Toward a theory of automatic information processing in reading. In H. Singer & R. B. Ruddell (Eds.). *Theoretical models and processes of reading* (3rd ed.) (pp. 689–721). Newark, DE: International Reading Association.

Lane, H. 1976. *The wild boy of Aveyron.* Cambridge, MA: Harvard University Press.

Larrick, N. (1983). A parent's guide to children's reading (5th ed.). Philadelphia: Westminster.

Lohnes, P. R., & Gray, M. M. (1972). Intellectual development and the Cooperative Reading Studies. *Reading Research Quarterly, 8,* 52–61.

Magoon, A. J. (1977). Constructivist approaches in educational research. *Review of Educational Research, 47,* 651–693.

Mathews, M. M. (1966). *Teaching to read: Historically considered.* Chicago: University of Chicago Press.

Moore, R. S., & Moore, D. N. (1977). *Better late than early: A new approach to your child's education.* New York: Reader's Digest Press.

Oakes, J. (1985). *Keeping track: How schools structure inequality.* New Haven, CT: Yale University Press.

Olson, W. C. (1959). *Child development* (2nd ed.). Boston: D. C. Heath.

Orton, J. (1966). The Orton-Gillingham approach. In J. Money (Ed.), *The disabled reader: Education of the dyslexic child* (pp. 119–146). Baltimore, MD: The Johns Hopkins Press.

Piaget, J. (1955). *The language and thought of the child.* New York: Meridian.

Piaget, J. (1985). *The equilibration of cognitive structures: The central problem of intellectual development.* (T. Brown & K. J. Thampy, Trans.). Chicago: University of Chicago Press.

Piaget, J., & Inhelder, B. (1969). *The psychology of the child.* New York: Basic Books.

Postman, N. (1982). *The disappearance of childhood.* New York: Dell.

Read, C. (1971). Pre-school children's knowledge of English phonology. *Harvard Educational Review, 41,* 1–34.

Reid, J. (1966). Learning to think about reading. *Educational Research, 9,* 56–62.

Ridgers, B. (1983). The identification and prevalence of specific reading retardation. *British Journal of Educational Psychology, 53,* 369–373.

Robinson, K., & Rudge, P. (1982). Centrally generated auditory potentials. In A. M. Halliday (Ed.)., *Evoked potentials in clinical testing.* London: Churchill Livingston.

Rosso, B. R., & Emans, R. (1981). Children's use of phonic generalizations. *The Reading Teacher, 34,* 653–658.

Rousseau, J. J. (1911). *Emile.* London: J. M. Dent. (Original work published 1762)

Shuy, R. (1981). A holistic view of language. *Research in the Teaching of English, 15,* 101–112.

Singer, H. (1985). The substrata-factor theory of reading. In H. Singer & R. B.

Ruddell (Eds.), *Theoretical models and processes of reading* (3rd ed.) (pp. 630–660). Newark, DE: International Reading Association.

Singer, H., & Ruddell, R. B. (Eds.). (1976). *Theoretical models and processes of reading* (2nd ed.). Newark, DE: International Reading Association.

Singer, H., & Ruddell, R. B. (Eds.). (1985). *Theoretical models and processes of reading* (3rd ed.). Newark, DE: International Reading Association.

Sirotnik, K. A. (1983). What you see is what you get: Consistency, persistency, and mediocrity in classrooms. *Harvard Educational Review, 53,* 16–31.

Smith, F. (1971). *Understanding reading: A psycholinguistic analysis of reading and learning to read* (1st ed.). New York: Holt, Rinehart & Winston.

Smith, F. (1978). *Reading without nonsense.* New York: Teachers College Press.

Smith, F. (1982). *Understanding reading: A psycholinguistic analysis of reading and learning to read* (3rd ed.). New York: Holt, Rinehart & Winston.

Spencer, P. L. (1961). The nature of the reading process and building balanced reading programs. In M. P. Douglass (Ed.), *Claremont Reading Conference, 25th yearbook* (pp. 1–10). Claremont, CA: The Claremont Graduate School.

Spencer, P. L. (1973). The Claremont Reading Conference: Its message and educational implications. In M. P. Douglass (Ed.), *Claremont Reading Conference, 37th yearbook* (pp. 205–215). Claremont, CA: The Claremont Graduate School.

Stedman, L. C., & Kaestle, C. F. (1987). Literacy and reading performance in the United States, from 1880 to the present. *Reading Research Quarterly, 22,* 8–46.

Thorndike, E. (1917). Reading as reasoning: A study of mistakes in paragraph reading. *Journal of Educational Psychology, 8,* 323–332.

Tovey, D. R. (1980). Children's grasp of phonics terms vs. sound-symbol relationships. *The Reading Teacher, 33,* 431–437.

Vernon, M. D. (1957). *Backwardness in reading.* Cambridge: Cambridge University Press.

Vygotsky, L. S. (1962). *Thought and language.* Cambridge, MA: MIT Press.

Wier, R. (1962). *Language in the crib.* The Hague: Mouton.

Yule, W., et al. (1974). Over and underachievement in reading; Distribution in the general population. *British Journal of Eductional Psychology, 44,* 1–11.

Index

About the Author

MALCOLM DOUGLASS is a professor of education at The Claremont Graduate School, where he has for a number of years been the Director of the Center for Developmental Studies in Education. One of his responsibilities in that regard has been oversight of the instructional program at the Mary B. Eyre Children's School, where early language curriculums have been developed based on the principles enunciated in this book. He also has played a central role in the development of the George G. Stone Center for Children's Books, a model library and research center for the study of children's literature and its applications in a school setting.

Professor Douglass is the long-time director of the Claremont Reading Conference, perhaps the most prestigious conference series devoted to the subject of reading, and is editor of its highly regarded annual publication, the *Claremont Reading Conference Yearbook*. The father of three grown children and two grandchildren, Professor Douglass resides in Claremont, California.